PATHWAYS TO INSTITUTIONAL IMPROVEMENT WITH INFORMATION TECHNOLOGY IN EDUCATIONAL MANAGEMENT

IFIP - The International Federation for Information Processing

IFIP was founded in 1960 under the auspices of UNESCO, following the First World Computer Congress held in Paris the previous year. An umbrella organization for societies working in information processing, IFIP's aim is two-fold: to support information processing within its member countries and to encourage technology transfer to developing nations. As its mission statement clearly states,

IFIP's mission is to be the leading, truly international, apolitical organization which encourages and assists in the development, exploitation and application of information technology for the benefit of all people.

IFIP is a non-profitmaking organization, run almost solely by 2500 volunteers. It operates through a number of technical committees, which organize events and publications. IFIP's events range from an international congress to local seminars, but the most important are:

- The IFIP World Computer Congress, held every second year;
- open conferences;
- working conferences.

The flagship event is the IFIP World Computer Congress, at which both invited and contributed papers are presented. Contributed papers are rigorously refereed and the rejection rate is high.

As with the Congress, participation in the open conferences is open to all and papers may be invited or submitted. Again, submitted papers are stringently refereed.

The working conferences are structured differently. They are usually run by a working group and attendance is small and by invitation only. Their purpose is to create an atmosphere conducive to innovation and development. Refereeing is less rigorous and papers are subjected to extensive group discussion.

Publications arising from IFIP events vary. The papers presented at the IFIP World Computer Congress and at open conferences are published as conference proceedings, while the results of the working conferences are often published as collections of selected and edited papers.

Any national society whose primary activity is in information may apply to become a full member of IFIP, although full membership is restricted to one society per country. Full members are entitled to vote at the annual General Assembly, National societies preferring a less committed involvement may apply for associate or corresponding membership. Associate members enjoy the same benefits as full members, but without voting rights. Corresponding members are not represented in IFIP bodies. Affiliated membership is open to non-national societies, and individual and honorary membership schemes are also offered.

PATHWAYS TO INSTITUTIONAL IMPROVEMENT WITH INFORMATION TECHNOLOGY IN EDUCATIONAL MANAGEMENT

IFIP TC3/WG3.7 Fourth International Working Conference on Information Technology in Educational Management
July 27–31, 2000, Auckland, New Zealand

Edited by

C.J. Patrick Nolan
Massey University
New Zealand

Alex C.W. Fung
Hong Kong Baptist University
China

Margaret A. Brown
Massey University
New Zealand

KLUWER ACADEMIC PUBLISHERS
BOSTON / DORDRECHT / LONDON

Distributors for North, Central and South America:
Kluwer Academic Publishers
101 Philip Drive
Assinippi Park
Norwell, Massachusetts 02061 USA
Telephone (781) 871-6600
Fax (781) 871-6528
E-Mail <kluwer@wkap.com>

Distributors for all other countries:
Kluwer Academic Publishers Group
Distribution Centre
Post Office Box 322
3300 AH Dordrecht, THE NETHERLANDS
Telephone 31 78 6392 392
Fax 31 78 6546 474
E-Mail <services@wkap.nl>

Electronic Services <http://www.wkap.nl>

Library of Congress Cataloging-in-Publication Data

IFIP TC3/WG3.7 (Conference) (2000: Auckland, N.Z.)
Pathways to institutional improvement with information technology in educational management : IFIP TC3/WG3.7 Fourth International Working Conference on Information Technology in Educational Management, July 27-31, 2000, Auckland, New Zealand / edited by C.J. Patrick Nolan, Alex C.W. Fung, Margaret A. Brown.
p. cm. — (International Federation for Information Processing; 71)
Includes bibliographical references.
ISBN 0-7923-7493-2
1. School management and organization—Data processing—Congresses. 2. Information technology—Congresses. I. Nolan, C.J. Patrick, 1942– II. Fung, Alex C.W., 1949– III. Brown, Margaret A., 1954– IV. Title. V. International Federation for Information Processing (Series); 71.

LB2806.17 .P38 2001
371.2'00285—dc21 2001038421

Printed on acid-free paper.

Printed in the United States of America.

CONTENTS

INTRODUCTION

Pathways in Context 1
C.J.P. Nolan, A.C.W. Fung and M.A. Brown

SECTION 1: Models for Supporting and Enhancing Professional Practice

Managing Assessment: Using Technology to Facilitate Change 13
G. Welsh

The Distance Ecological Model to Support Self/Collaborative-Learning in the Internet Environment 21
T. Okamoto

Educational Centres as Knowledge Organisations Training Future Knowledge Workers: The Role of IT 31
J. Osorio, C. Zárraga and J. Rodríguez

SECTION 2: CSIS Models and Designs

Developing Software for School Administration and Management 45
M. Bajec, M. Krisper and R. Rupnik

Open ITEM Systems are Good ITEM Systems 59
A. Tatnall and B. Davey

Information Systems for Leading and Managing Schools: Changing the Paradigm 71
C.J.P. Nolan and M. Lambert

CSIS Usage in School Management: A Comparison of Good and Bad Practice Schools 87
A.J. Visscher and P.P.M. Bloemen

SECTION 3: Evaluation of System Effects

Has a Decade of Computerisation Made a Difference in School Management? 99
P. Wild, D. Smith and J. Walker

SAMS in Hong Kong Schools: A User Acceptance Audit........ 121
A.C.W. Fung and J. Ledesma

SECTION 4: Making a Difference Through Training and Professional Development

How Should School Managers Be Trained for Managerial School Information System Usage? 147
A.J. Visscher and E.M. Branderhorst

Supporting UK Teachers Through The National Grid for Learning........ 159
I. Selwood, D. Smith and J. Wisehart

Pathways in Context

C.J.P. Nolan, A.C.W. Fung and M.A. Brown

1. BACKGROUND

The contents of this book comprise peer refereed papers selected from the proceedings of the Fourth IFIP (International Federation for Information Processing) Working Conference of Working Group 3.7 on Information Technology and Educational Management (ITEM), held between July 28-30, 2000 in Auckland, New Zealand. Preceded by similar conferences in Israel (1994), Hong Kong (1996) and Maine, USA (1998), the 2000 Conference in New Zealand brought together diverse people and presentations that refined and expanded upon the findings of previous conferences. It added to them new findings from ongoing research and it made suggestions regarding possible new directions that computerised information system developments in education might take in the future to support improvement initiatives in schools and other educational institutions.

The focus on improvement emerged almost naturally out of the work of the previous conferences of Working Group 3.7 and, in response to the emerging needs of educational institutions generally, but especially schools. A key need is for computerised information systems that directly support activities and processes central to their operation professionally, technically and in managerial and leadership terms. That is to say, systems are now required that will increasingly permit the broad range of professionals (teachers, department heads, support staff and others) to routinely access and use computerised systems. They need such access and use to support curriculum delivery, the making of strategic decisions about learning and teaching, the monitoring and reporting of student progress and the enactment of a wide range of programme review, planning and policy implementation tasks. Fulmer (1995) earlier described both the developments and the needs they would help to meet as constitutive of work in the "technical core" of schools, *i.e.* curriculum enactment, learning and teaching and evaluation. The work of writers and researchers in IFIP Working Group 3.7 (*e.g.* Frank and Fulmer, 1998 and Nolan and Lambert, 2001) has since explored this emerging new conception of the use of computerised systems. They locate it in the larger mainstream trend towards the democratisation of school leadership, management and administration. Such a trend reflects, in its turn, the findings of school development and improvement theory and research (Fullan, 1993; Stewart, 2000). The findings identify ways not only that school management and leadership, but also school performance itself can be enhanced through the active engagement of the full range of school personnel in setting policy and in making decisions using computers.

In this respect, the papers selected for this volume constitute a further stage both in the development of computerised information systems for education (and particularly schools) and in our thinking about the possible form and content of such systems in the future. It could be said that system developments and our thinking have progressed through four stages that coincide with each of the ITEM conferences to date.

2. CONTEXT

Stage 1 centred around the first (1994) ITEM working Conference in Israel (Barta, *et al.*,1995) Here, the main emphasis was on *frameworks for conceiving, designing and implementing computerised systems*. This was at a time when two notions predominated. Firstly, the notion of computer assisted school administration (CASA) placed school administrators and the administrative office of schools at centre stage. Secondly, information technology and educational management was being established as a new field of professional activity, development and research in education (Fulmer *et al.*, 1998). Even at the Israel Conference, though, the concept of computerised school information system (CSIS) was being developed as a broader and more inclusive conception with which to inform development and guide practitioners' understanding of how computer technology might support administrative and management processes in and outside the administrative office.

In 1994, the shift in thinking among developers, researchers and practitioners from exclusive, closed-system designs to inclusive open-system designs had not yet fully occurred. The frameworks presented at that conference (*e.g.* Visscher, 1995) were sufficiently broad in scope and conceptually flexible, however, to accommodate the developments that were to follow and to guide their form and function.

The guiding influence of the frameworks is reflected, for instance, in Fulmer's (1995) theoretical construct of a "good system" which specified key attributes necessary to "collect data, automate processes and informate the work of multiple decision makers from different organisational levels" (Fulmer, *op cit.* p.7). The attributes are multiple input ports, alternative units of analysis for inquiry, variable types of data, choice of analytic processes and variable access ports for the retrieval of data. Today, most state of the art systems embody these criteria in their designs, range of functionality and operational capabilities. Four such systems were illustrated four years later in the developers workshop for school practitioners at the 1998 ITEM Conference in Maine, with findings reported in the Proceedings (Nolan, *et al.* 1998). These systems were integrated systems and a wide range of school personnel is increasingly using them routinely for higher order school development activities such as strategic planning, school review and programme design. This does not gainsay the fact that the predominant pattern continues: Computerised information system use remains confined to the administrative office. None the less, a new emerging pattern is also evident. Capable, dedicated and technically proficient practitioners increasingly use computer technology to improve and support learning and teaching, enhance programme design and encourage exemplary professional practice.

Stage 2 centred on the Hong Kong Conference (Fung, *et al.*, 1997) which, by and large, focussed upon *the functionality and use of systems and upon conditions that support use.* Importantly, however, the Conference in Hong Kong also symbolised the coming of age of Information Technology and Educational Management (ITEM) as a professional entity. It was established as Working Group 3.7 of the International Federation of Information Processing (IFIP) with a mandate to develop a professional and research community, *i.e.* effectively a community of scholars whose predominant interest is research and development in the emerging new field of ITEM. The members of the community would conduct research, employ the findings of research to inform new developments and produce scholarly outputs for both specialist and general audiences (Nolan and Visscher, 1996). Thus, while the focus of many presentations at Hong Kong was on functionality and use, the broad mandate of the newly formed ITEM Working Group served as a catalyst for development in other directions. This was because the formal mandate of ITEM WG 3.7 was to address not just the development, implementation and use of computerised systems. It was also mandated to address issues and topics related to the context of use, to social and normative aspects such as access and equity and to emerging new conceptions of computerised systems.

Such a mandate was timely in 1996 because by then papers presented at the Hong Kong Conference signaled an emerging new trend in thinking about computerised systems. This was towards managing and integrating information with the technology and the new trend identified in 1996 set the scene for the next Conference scheduled for Maine in 1998.

Principally for this reason the *Integration of Information for Educational Management* became the theme for the 1998 ITEM Working Conference in Maine and this conference accordingly became the hub of Stage 3. It was preceded in the period between conferences by a concerted effort to publish and disseminate to the wider community of educational practitioners and researchers the collective contemporary findings of ongoing research in the field of information technology and educational management. These were contained in a special edition of the *International Journal of Educational Research* (Visscher 1996) which accurately represented developments in the field, and the predominant focus of computerised system developments around functionality, implementation, use and integration. Visscher (1996) attempted to embody all of this in a single unified and comprehensive *School Information System Framework.* Vigorous debate ensued, and continues to this day, between Visscher and protagonists (*e.g.*, Fung, 1996; Visscher, Fung and Wild, 1998) and others in WG 3.7 (*e.g.*, Nolan and Ayres 1996, Frank and Fulmer 1998, Nolan and Lambert 2001) about the adequacy of the Framework. In particular, they debated its adequacy to accommodate an emerging new conception of the school as a learning community (Nolan and Lambert, *op cit.*) as opposed to organisation in the somewhat Weberian sense in which Visscher conceives organisation. The debate indicates the healthy intellectual climate of the Group and it reflects also the commitment of the Group to the norms of collaborative, collegial and reflective practice.

Participants at the 1996 Conference took seriously their wider mandate to address the full spectrum of topics and issues with which practitioners, developers and researchers alike were concerned, or might be concerned in the future. By 1998, a new generation of computerised information systems for schools in particular were available for practitioner use. They were systems with far greater "connectivity" than in the past, in the sense of programes for linking and analysing disparate data and information and for permitting access by mutliple users. That is, they were designed to make practitioner access and use more democratic in the manner previously mentioned (Nolan *et al.*, 1998). The systems could, for instance, generate what Fulmer and Frank (1998) referred to as "teacher valued data" and teachers could access the data and process it in the classroom. In this way, the locus of control over computerised school information system use could be decentralised and teachers thereby permitted to generate and analyse data and information useful to them.

Herein lay the germ of an idea for the theme of the ITEM2000 New Zealand Conference: *Institutional Improvement through Information Technology in Educational Management.* While not expressed using these words in 1998, the tenor and conclusions of many papers (notably, Frank and Fulmer 1998, Nolan *et al.*, 1998 and Tatnall and Tatnall, 1998) indicated a newly emerging concern. This was to address the impact and effects of computerised systems on students and teachers and upon learning and teaching. As one school administrator commented in 1998 during the demonstration of new state of the art systems "the technology being presented to us now, such as *Classroom Manager*, (an integrated, multifunctional application especially designed for teacher use), is pioneering the way. It could be that we are going to see an absolute explosion in the next ten years in how information can be used in planning, how we spend money, how to arrange classes, and how to plan for the different educational needs of girls and boys" (Maine Elementary Principal, Fulmer, *et al.*, 1998).

Such comment represents a commitment to school improvement as a predominant professional norm of the schools and the teaching profession. More importantly, it represents the mind set of teachers and school administrators that expenditure of scarce school finances on computerised school information systems ultimately is justified in two ways. Firstly, a computerised system can enhance school administration and management at all levels so that overall the school generally operates more smoothly and efficiently with respect to organisational and administrative aspects. Secondly, teacher and administrator use of the system contributes directly to ongoing improvements in learning and teaching, perhaps through improved curriculum planning, better monitoring of student achievement and progress and more effective use of teacher time for teaching and professional development.

At the 2000 Conference, the participants took seriously their responsibility to address the nominated theme of the Conference – the improvement of schools and other educational institutions. And in this way, the focus on improvement symbolised the engagement of WG 3.7 and its dominant concern in Stage 4. Diversity has always been a defining characteristic of WG 3.7, however, and the participants (much smaller in number than at previous conferences, though no less diverse) interpreted the theme in markedly different ways that reflected the diversity of their interests in ITEM and their diverse backgrounds in nine different countries. The countries included Australia, China, England, Japan, New Zealand, The Netherlands, The Philippines, Spain and Slovenia. The professional and institutional backgrounds of the participants encompassed school administration, primary and secondary teaching, policy making, research covering systems engineering, business studies, computers in education, software development, and school information system development and design and school advisory roles.

3. STRUCTURE

The Chapters in this book, peer refereed internationally by members of the IFIP, W.G. 3.7 programme committee of the Conference, are representative of the distinctive ways that participants addressed the conference theme of school and institutional improvement through the implementation and use of computerised information systems, for education. The contents are in four sections summarised below.

3.1 Models for supporting and enhancing professional practice

Contemporary research documents a key role that information technology can, and increasingly does, play in fostering collaborative and productive practice in schools and other educational institutions. Three chapters in Section 1 elaborate on this role for information technology. Two of them (Welsh and Okamoto) describe and examine two models comprising interactive information technology designs for supporting specific aspects of teachers' professional practice. Welsh reports on an IT System for managing the assessment of student learning, developed by teachers in a group of New Zealand secondary schools. Okamoto reports a distance education model within which collaborative communication permits school based curriculum development and teacher training. While the focus of both systems is on support for, and the enhancement of, professional practice, elements within both chapters complement chapters in Section 4 on training and professional development. In a somewhat different vein, the third chapter by Osorio, Zarraga and Rodriguez proposes a collaborative IT framework for educational centres (especially schools and universities) with responsibility for the education of "future knowledge workers". They argue that if educators, and education, are to keep in touch with the social and professional realities for which students are destined, then educational centres must fundamentally changes their missions. In particular, they must change from being providers and disseminators of educational knowledge to being teachers of knowledge management skills that increasingly are commonplace in and valued by, businesses and corporations. To do this, educational centres must collaborate and work more in partnership with, rather than isolation from, the business and corporate community.

3.2 CSIS models and designs

In the past, computerised information systems commonly were built for the benefit of central educational authorities rather than schools, with the result that many of the systems were inflexible and fail to meet many of the needs of the schools. Such systems tended to address ways of meeting external accountability requirements. They were less than helpful in assisting school managers and administrators to administer their schools internally and to support, in-house, such key school development tasks as curriculum design, the evaluation of programmes and the recording and reporting of student achievement. The chapters in Section 2 identify and examine the characteristics of 'good' computerised school information systems. Additionally, they challenge conventional views about what constitutes a good system. Bajec, Krisper and Rupnik argue that value lies in the application of a Business Rules approach to achieve flexible management and administration system designs, thereby permitting adaptability of use in diverse educational settings. Tatnall and Davies present a case for the development of open systems. This development would be in the direction of system designs that permit users to adapt their systems for specific purposes and integrate new kinds of "third party products" that may either extend the functionality of a given system or change its character. Nolan and Lambert argue that, with schools of the future operating more as learning communities than as organisations, then computerised school information systems designs must increasingly embody design precepts and principles broader than the organisationally orientated spreadsheet designs that currently predominate. Visscher and Bloemen suggest that systems of the future will enable school improvement to the extent that they provide school managers and leaders with tools for autonomous and strategic decision making. The case study they report operationalises a distinction between 'good' and 'bad' practice that managers and administrators employ in supporting staff use of computerised school information systems.

3.3 Evaluation of system effects

In the last ten years, a very rapid growth in the number and range of computerised information systems for schools and educational organisations has occurred worldwide. Research is only now being completed which addresses the extent to which computerised systems actually enhance administrative and management practices in education and render them more efficient and effective. The chapters in Section 3 report findings from studies of computerised systems that have been widely adopted and used by school systems in two countries, the SIMS (School Information Management System) system in England and SAMS (School Administration and Management System) in Hong Kong, China. While both studies report that the systems contributed to increased administrative efficiency, they also report on limits to effective adoption and use due notably to the relative lack of appropriate and timely professional development and support for users. This factor has been identified elsewhere as vital to successful uptake, adoption and utilisation (Nolan, *et al.*, 2001).

3.4 Making a Difference through training and professional development

The research by Nolan, *et al.* (2001), referred to above, indicates that the timeliness and appropriateness of professional development and training must in the first instance be linked to user concerns and provided in response to them. It must be sensitive to context and be conducted at a pace and in ways that develop confidence and competency progressively. The position taken by Visscher and Branderhorst is that few professional development and training systems exist or are in use that satisfies all of these criteria. They identify and examine the characteristics of effective training systems for school managers. In contrast, Selwood, Smith and Wisehart examine the effectiveness of the National Grid for Learning, which is a British developed Internet-based system for the training and support of school staff in the use of a wide range of IT tools from classroom teaching and learning to school office. The system comprises a "mosaic of interconnecting networks and education services... which supports teaching, learning, training and administration in schools, colleges, universities, libraries, the work place and homes". The system is, in effect, a comprehensive and potentially far reaching, on-line communications network. The effectiveness of its use depends, however, on user access to timely, appropriate and ongoing professional development and training.

In all sections, the chapters address in varying ways the general theme of institutional improvement through and with information technology in educational management - ITEM. The theme reflects, in its turn, the general focus and direction of contemporary mainstream educational and school development research. There, practitioners and researchers alike now acknowledge that, in order to be useful, research and development must be capable of yielding outcomes (insights, understandings and operational principles) that can inform, perhaps change, the thinking and professional judgment of educational practitioners. In this way research and development such as that reported in this book might enhance conditions for effective learning and teaching in schools and in the wider education community encompassing agencies and organisations as diverse as early childhood education centres to universities.

The 1998 Conference in Maine, USA included a developer's workshop. Its purpose was to develop the nexus between practitioners (*i.e.* the users of systems and consumers of research), system developers and designers and researchers. In many respects, the workshop was a highlight of the Conference. This is reflected in the sense of excitement and wonderment reported in the Preface to the Proceedings at what had already been accomplished with information technology, and at what might be accomplished in the near future. In the concluding chapter, Nolan *et al.* (1998) commented that uptake and use of computerised systems could founder if two conditions are not present. The first is practitioners seeing value in the systems as a means to support and enhance teaching and the learning of children and students. The second is the presence and the development of school and institutional cultures that support innovations such as computerised information systems.

These observations are worth reiterating here in light of a bold new initiative in the Philippines called TAO CARES (Computer Assisted Reforms for Schools) project, outlined in a Conference 2000 presentation by Senator Teresa Aquino-Oreta (Chairperson, Senate Committee on Education, Arts and Culture), though not formally reported here. TAO CARES is a centrally funded Government project which, on the face of it, combines features of both top-down, mandated system developments (Fung, *et al.*, 2001) with bottom-up developments whose mandate is practitioner and school needs and priorities. In the case of the Philippines, it is possible that its two-pronged strategy may result in avoidance of the many pitfalls commonly associated with top-down mandated developments (*e.g.*, user avoidance or rejection). At the same time, it may secure user commitment through engagement of users, and prospective users, in the development, design and piloting process (Nolan, Brown and Graves, 2001).

In a sense, the report on TAO CARES by Aquino-Oreta corresponded with the developers workshop in Maine, 1998. It did so in the sense that the Philippines initiative has the potential to bring together developers, educational practitioners and researchers to form a nexus in the Philippines and with significant others from elsewhere. This could generate design and development, adoption, implementation and utilisation strategies and solutions in a way that has hitherto not happened in other countries. The Philippines' initiative reflects an attitude of optimism and hope for the future, tempered by realism. It is laudable given the contemporary political upheaval of the Philippines and the conditions of impoverishment and system-wide lacks of resources endemic in Philippines society generally and in its school and education system, in particular. Nonetheless, the initiators of the TAO CARES project are determined and they understand more than their predecessors in other countries about what must, and can be done to bring about change. Perhaps the presentation on TAO CARES foreshadows the next stage of development for ITEM and its Working Group 3.7 in the International Federation for Information Processing (IFIP). This might be called the Stage 5 - Empowerment: Educational practitioners controlling and using modern computer technology both to lead and manage education and to develop schools as "public good" institutions supporting equity in education and providing educational opportunity for all.

Editors
Pat Nolan
Alex Fung
Margaret Brown

ACKNOWLEDGEMENTS

The editors would especially like to thank Philippa Butler for her work as proof reader and Anneke Visser for her typesetting work.

REFERENCES

Barta, B., Telem, M.& Gev, Y. (Eds.) (1995) *Information technology in educational management.* London: Chapman & Hall.

Fullan, M.G. (1992). *Successful school improvement: The implementation perspective and beyond.* Buckingham: Open University Press.

Fulmer, C.L. (1995) Maximising the potential of information technology for management strategies for interfacing the technical core of education. In B.Z. Barta, M. Telem, & Y. Gev (Eds.), *Information technology in educational management.* London: Chapman Hall.

Frank, E.P., & Fulmer, C.L. (1998). The dysfunctional side of educational organizations: Themes from clinical information system development. In C.Fulmer, B.Barta,& P.Nolan (Eds.), *The integration of information for educational management.* Whitefield, ME: Felicity Press.

Fung, A.C.W. & Ledesma,J. (2001). SAMS in Hong Kong schools: A user acceptance audit. In C.J.P. Nolan, A.C.W. Fung, & M.A. Brown (Eds.), *Pathways to institutional improvement with information technology in educational management.* London: Kluwer.

Fung, A.C.W., Visscher, A.J., Barta, B., & Teather, D.C.B. (1997). *Information technology in educational management for the schools of the future.* London: Chapman and Hall.

Fung, A.C.W. (1996). An evaluation of the Hong Kong design and development strategy. *International Journal of Educational Research, 25* (40), 297-305.

Nolan, C.J.P., & Ayres, D.A. (1996). Developing a "good" information for schools: The New Zealand experience. *International Journal of Educational Research, 25* (5), 307-319.

Nolan, C.J.P. and Visscher, A.J. (1996). Research on information technology in educational management. In J.D. Tinsley and T.J. van Weert (Eds.), *Post-conference report on the Sixth IFIP World Conference on Computers in Education*. Birmingham: IFIP Technical Committee 3.

Nolan, C.J.P., Fulmer, C.L., & Taylor, R. (1998).Four computerized school information systems: Summary discussion. In C. Fulmer, B. Barta, & P. Nolan (Eds.), *The integration of information for educational management.* London: Kluwer.

Nolan, C.J.P., Brown, M.A., & Graves, B. (2001). MUSAC in New Zealand: From grass roots to system-wide in a decade. In A.J. Visscher, P. Wild, and A.C.W. Fung (Eds.), *Information technology in educational management: School information systems in the 21st century*. The Netherlands: Kluwer.

Nolan, C.J.P., & Lambert, M. (2001). Information systems for leading and managing schools: Changing the paradigm. In C.J.P. Nolan, A.C.W. Fung, & M.A. Brown (Eds.), *Pathways to institutional improvement with information technology in educational management.* London: Kluwer.

Stewart, D. (2000). *Tomorrow's principals today*. Palmerston North: Dunmore Print.

Tatnall, A & Tatnall, B. (1998). Data integration in a training institute: Modelling a client-server solution. In C.L. Fulmer, B.Z. Barta, & P. Nolan (Eds.), *The integration of information for educational management.* Whitefield, Maine: Felicity Press.

Visscher, A. J. (1995). Computer assisted school administration and management: Where we are and where should we go? In B. Barta, M. Telem & Y. Gev (Eds.), *Information technology in educational management.* London: Chapman & Hall.

Visscher, A.J. (1996). The implications of how staff handle information for the usage of school information systems. *International Journal of Educational Research, 25* (4), 323-334.

Visscher, A.J., Fung, A.C.W., & Wild, P. (1999). The evaluation of the large scale implementation of a computer-assisted management information system in Hong Kong schools. *Studies in Educational Evaluation, 25,* 11-31.

1

Managing Assessment: Using Technology to Facilitate Change

G. Welsh
Massey University, College of Education, Centre for Educational Development, Palmerston North, New Zealand

Key words: Computerised School Information Systems, Professional Development, Assessment, Effective School Development

Abstract: This paper describes a number of developments focusing on school-wide assessment, recording and reporting. Such factors as secondary school culture and change, the external pressures to comply, and action research elements are considered. Discussion of findings from these projects reveal: (1) the influential role that computer software can play in collaborative developments, and (2) the relationship between software system implementation and cultural change. This suggests ways that CSIS could be more productively used to assist with school development.

1. INTRODUCTION

The evolution of computerised school information systems (CSIS) in New Zealand secondary schools has been characterised by an emphasis on the automation, and quest to improve efficiency, of administrative processes. The emerging challenge is to utilise the power of the microprocessor to promote and facilitate school developments that impact positively on student achievement. This may necessitate a re-examination of the established, and often disparate, functions of professional development services and CSIS providers.

2. BACKGROUND

New Zealand schools have experienced unprecedented change during the last decade. Radical restructuring of the frameworks for both curriculum and qualifications followed a movement towards self-management in 1989. The curriculum framework, consisting of seven essential learning areas, has been progressively introduced with completion not expected until 2002. The new Qualifications Framework, based on unit standards, was launched in 1994.

The introduction of unit standards signalled an emphatic movement towards the use of internal assessment for awarding qualifications at the senior secondary school level. Each course had unit standards defined, which described the outcomes and the performance criteria that would be used to determine whether or not the standard had been achieved. Approximately five to eight standards would be used for each full year course and each standard had a number of credits associated with it. The plan, which has since been modified, was for these credits to contribute to a National Certificate of Educational Achievement, at years 12 and 13, and other, subject specific, National Certificates.

Secondary schools were faced with the task of recording and reporting unit standard results to the New Zealand Qualifications Authority[1]. This, by itself, was not a major issue as the significant suppliers of CSIS had modules available which satisfied this need. At this time a model was being presented to school audiences demonstrating how the recording, reporting and evaluation of assessment data, relating to the curriculum framework, could be relatively straight forward IF there was a common assessment 'currency' across the school. This model was converted into software form for demonstration purposes. However, the staggered introduction of curriculum statements for each of the essential learning areas, and their Maori equivalents, meant that schools were not ready to tackle whole-school implementation issues. Several school managers believed that this software model could be applied in an area where there was already an established school-wide assessment currency: unit standards.

Thirty-five secondary schools are currently involved with the unit standard component of this development. Thirteen secondary schools, most of whom also belong to the first group, are part of a more extensive project with the goal of improving student achievement by developing an approach to assessment in secondary schools based on standards and emphasising the essential role that formative assessment can play. In many, but not all, of the schools belonging to the second group, unit standards have served as a lever

[1] The New Zealand Qualifications Authority is a Crown Entity established to co-ordinate national qualifications.

to introduce a similar approach to assessment in the junior school. This paper is a commentary on developments involving schools from the second group.

Participation in these professional and school development projects is voluntary – schools may join or leave at any time. The schools vary in size from a little over 100 students to over 1000 with a mode of approximately 700 students. The junior division of these schools generally refers to years 9 and 10, or students in the 13-15 age group. All participating schools utilise the MUSAC[2] school information system and, in particular, the MUSAC *Pupil Files* program which is used to manage student personal data.

Although essentially self-managing, schools must comply with several sets of guidelines promulgated by the Ministry of Education (MOE). One of these guidelines, National Administration Guideline 1, or NAG1 as it is commonly called, refers to the collection and utilisation of assessment data based on the curriculum objectives contained in the national curriculum statements for each essential learning area. The Education Review Office[3] uses the guidelines to audit school compliance and, to a limited extent, school performance. Many, if not most, secondary schools have had difficulty in satisfying NAG1 and, consequently, ERO. Typical expressions included in the ERO generated audit reports[4] for secondary schools include:

- Implementation of an agreed school-wide system should enable the school to improve evaluation of student progress;
- The school is knowledgeable about the significance of assessment but has still to decide what is best practice for school-wide adoption; and
- The school needs to face the challenge of reviewing its approaches to assessment, recording and reporting, and develop systems that enable it to demonstrate student progress more effectively.

Secondary schools operate in a competitive environment with increasing student mobility contributing to significant fluctuation in school rolls. The public nature of the ERO reports therefore provides a strong motivation for action to address non-compliance issues, in particular. Most of the schools participating in these professional and school development projects derived their initial impetus in this way.

[2] Massey University School Administration by Computer (MUSAC) software is used extensively in a large number of New Zealand schools and is continually evolving to meet the needs of a rapidly changing educational environment. Refer to the MUSAC website at http://musac.massey.ac.nz

[3] The Education Review Office (ERO) is the government department which reports publicly on the quality of education in all New Zealand schools and early childhood centres, including private schools, kura kaupapa Maori (Maori language immersion schools), special schools and kohanga reo (Maori language early childhood groups).

[4] These reports are available from http://www.ero.govt.nz

The method used for these school developments varied according to the size of the schools and their state of readiness. However, the use of several in-school workshops for the whole staff (small school) or curriculum representatives (larger school) has been common. These workshops have covered:

- Issues surrounding the implementation of the curriculum framework;
- The need for transparency from assessment to reporting;
- Formative assessment and reporting;
- Agreement on the desirability of a common assessment currency and what this should be;
- Possibilities for the aggregation and analysis of achievement data – will it lead to better programmes and learning?;
- The benefits of school-wide consistency; and
- A means of achieving this.

The use of CSIS to promote consistent approaches to assessment was to be an essential feature (see James, 1998).

3. USING CSIS TO FACILITATE CHANGE

Progressing with these projects meant overcoming significant barriers. Autonomous subject departments in secondary schools, the staggered introduction of curriculum statements, and the legacy of decades of reliance on external examinations have been the most prominent obstacles. The software developed to support these projects has played an integral part, not only in helping teachers conceptualise the underpinning model, but in actually implementing their developmental plans. It is a collaborative development with all participating schools and is continually evolving as our experiences with and knowledge of assessment, reporting and evaluation expands.

Table 1. The evolving software

Program characteristic	Evolutionary rationale
Networkability	As the reporting aspect gained momentum, simultaneous access by a number of staff was enabled.
Portability of data	Constraints on teachers' in-school time created a need to export or import subsets of data to be used on a remote workstation. As well as maintaining the integrity of the database, issues such as low machine memory and speed of the remote workstations needed to be addressed.
Ease of use	Teachers bring with them a range of experiences and skills, and unnecessary complexity or procedures discourages rather than facilitates the utilisation of CSIS.
Security and backup	Experience demanded that multiple backup scenarios were built in, *e.g.* automatically saving data when a window was closed. Password protection was needed to maintain global configuration integrity.
Limited flexibility	It transpired that there needed to be a balance between flexibility (to allow for departmental or school peculiarities) and the use of 'constants' (to emphasis the desired assessment model and ensure school-wide consistency).
Reporting	The ability to generate reports directly from assessment data was an important principle, which was incorporated.
Data entry	Apart from report comments (which can be automated) this is achieved, though not exclusively, through mouse manipulation. A compromise needed to be made between data complexity and ease of use.
Compatibility	Data transfer from MUSAC or other systems is seamless and automatic.
Evaluation/analysis of data	This is at a formative stage as schools come to terms with a school-wide assessment 'currency' and the use of the available technology tools.[5]
Year to year continuity	The facility to archive reports and assessment information generally was anticipated. This does present some issues, however[6].

The temptation to develop a flexible open-ended program needed to be tempered with the current state of computer literacy among secondary school teachers. As Ayres, Nolan and Visscher (1998) point out, senior managers and administration staff are the major users of CSIS, predominantly for administrative purposes. There appears to be a direct relationship between the flexibility of and the complexity of the software used in this context. A conscious decision was therefore made to restrict the flexibility in an attempt

[5] Described by Nolan, Fulmer and Taylor (1998) as moving from data management to information management.

[6] Frank and Fulmer (1998) explain that multi-level data is very powerful but can also be very condemning.

to maximise ease of use. There exists no obvious impediment, from a data structure perspective, to the adoption of a more sophisticated open-ended system once the development objectives have been achieved.

There is no escaping the need to report to caregivers or parents and most schools demand consistency in the manner in which this is done. The generation of computerised reports, unavoidable in the context of these projects, provided a useful focus for the up-skilling of teachers in the use of CSIS. This up-skilling was managed through peer facilitation with little external input. One difficulty faced was the tendency to unduly focus on the format and layout of a report rather than the content. This has not been overcome in all schools but the use of trials, targeting specific curriculum areas or year levels, and the subsequent process of diffusion shows promise.

The software has played an invaluable role in motivating participants but, like other school development projects, essential components of change management also need to feature – strong internal leadership, a culture accepting of change, and a value placed on Professional Development. Predominant variables and the pace of change vary significantly from school to school. Identification of the factors contributing to this has not revealed anything beyond what contemporary research in this domain tells us, but contextualising is helping schools to understand their own complex culture and plan for successful change.

Table 2. Summary of progress to-date and cultural characteristics

Status	Characteristics
Stuck on first base	Predominantly academically focused (the school and/or the managers and/or the community), with an emphasis on external examinations. Hierarchical management structure not predisposed to grass-roots development. An emphasis on compliance rather than on development (often for reasons of work-load). Project capture by teacher(s) with specific curriculum bias.
Deliberating on third base	Some strongly independent, autonomous subject departments. Smaller school where work-load is not easily shared. Taking a breather – change can be energy sapping. Cautionary movement anticipating further, alternative rather than progressive, change.
Home run!	Flexible and innovative approach to professional development. Purposeful, informed and shared leadership. Change as the norm rather than as the exception. Collaborative problem solving approach out of necessity (survival in a competitive environment) rather than for intrinsic benefit. Resident technical expertise for trouble-shooting purposes.

4. SUMMARY

Most of the software currently utilised in secondary schools has been designed along traditional lines and has not changed significantly[7], user interface/operating system and functionality excepted, over the last decade (see Nolan, Fulmer and Taylor, 1998). The small New Zealand market possibly inhibits extensive research and development in this area. Consequently, schools have had to fit the system which is contrary to what Nolan & Lambert (2001) report as being necessary for the proper utilisation of CSIS. The software used in these school projects has been developed collaboratively and in parallel with the professional development programme. The progress made can be attributable, in no small way, to the use of CSIS tools to model ideas, overcome workload issues and handle the complexity involved in collating student learning outcomes from diverse curriculum areas. Bringing separate subject departments, often with their own divergent approaches, together has been an essential phase of this development relying heavily on the purpose built software.

The computer programs that have evolved out of these school developments have been designed to complement rather than compete with commercially produced software. The focus has been on whole-school development. When attempting to devise solutions with open-ended CSIS, schools have effectively been left to their own devices. External software support is confined to 'training in the use of' and schools receive no support, from this source, with the underpinning philosophies, rationale and implications. In fact, a number of schools in this region have re-invented antiquated systems for reporting under the guise of 'progressive' computerisation. Schools ostensibly faced with the same challenges (in relation to NAG1) have reacted in many different ways with quite diverse outcomes. These outcomes, or developments, rely very much on the style of internal leadership and the nature of the 'resident' technological expertise.

These projects are dynamic in the sense that each milestone achieved induces investigative urges and the formulation of fresh objectives. One school, through the principle co-ordinator, has recently completed an action research study on the impact that this project has had on teacher planning, assessment methodology and, not surprisingly, student achievement.

[7] MUSAC's *Classroom Manager* promises to contradict this.

5. IMPLICATIONS

Professional Development and software support for schools have been treated as different entities, provided by different organisations and funded from different sources. For significant developments involving technology tools, such as those described here, this is not necessary or even desirable. An analogous comparison could be made with the beneficial process of linking learning and assessment more closely. The emerging concept is therefore the utility of merging the functions of external professional development and CSIS support as a means of enabling effective school development.

There is potential to generate 'indigenous' research through collaborative projects 'owned' by the school. If the ultimate goal is to raise student achievement then schools need to develop the capacity to find out whether this has happened. The willingness, and capacity, to conduct indigenous research should be strongly encouraged as it indubitably enhances the school development process.

REFERENCES

Ayers, D., Nolan, C.J.P., & Visscher, A.J. (1998). Computerised school information systems: Researching New Zealand usage patterns and levels of use. In C. Fulmer, B. Barta, & P. Nolan (Eds.), *The integration of information for educational management*. Whitefield, ME: Felicity Press.

Frank, F.P., & Fulmer, C.L. (1998). The dysfunctional side of educational organisations: Themes from clinical information system development. In C. Fulmer, B. Barta, & P. Nolan (Eds.), *The integration of information for educational management*. Whitefield, ME: Felicity Press.

James, M. (1998). *Using assessment for school improvement*. Oxford: Heinemann Educational Press.

Nolan, C.J.P., & Lambert, M. (2001). Information systems for leading and managing schools: Changing the paradigm. In P. Nolan & A. Fung (Eds.), *Institutional improvement through information technology in educational management*. London: Kluwer.

Nolan, C.J.P., Fulmer, C.L., & Taylor, R. (1998). Four computerised school information systems: Summary discussion. In C. Fulmer, B. Barta, & P. Nolan (Eds.), *The integration of information for educational management*. Whitefield, ME: Felicity Press.

Education Review Office (2000). *School audit reports*. Wellington: ERO. [http://www.ero.govt.nz]

Ministry of Education (1999). *The national administration guidelines* (revised). Wellington: Ministry of Education.

2

The Distance Ecological Model to Support Self/Collaborative-Learning in the Internet Environment

T. Okamoto
University of Electro-Communications, Graduate School of Information Systems, 1-5-1 Chofugaoka Chofu-shi Tokyo, 182-8585 Japan

Key words: Distance Education, Teacher Training System, Distance Educational Model, Learning Ecology, School Based Curriculum Development, Training System

Abstract: With the rapid development of information technology, computer and information communication literacy has become extremely important. As a result, teachers require new skills. A new teachers' education framework is necessary to enhance multimedia teaching skills and information literacy about the Internet environment. The purpose of this study is to propose and develop a Distance Educational Model, which is a School-Based Curriculum Development and Training-System (SCOUTS). In this environment, a teacher can learn subject contents, teaching knowledge, and evaluation methods of students' learning activities, related to the new subject called "Information", via an Internet based self-training system. In this paper, we describe the structure, function and mechanism of the Distance Educational Model, and then describe the educational meaning of this model in consideration of the new learning ecology, which is based on multi-modality and new learning situations and forms.

1. INTRODUCTION

Recently, with the development of information and communication technologies, various teaching methods using Internet, multimedia, and so on, are being introduced. Most of these methods emphasise, in particular, the aspect of collaborative communication between students and teacher during interactive teaching and learning activities. Therefore, now-a-days it is extremely important for a teacher to acquire computer communication literacy (Nishinosono, 1998).

So far, there have been many studies concerning system development, which aim at fostering and expanding teachers' practical abilities and comprehensive teaching skills by using new technologies, such as computers, Internet, multimedia, and so on. In Japan, systems using communication satellites such as SCS (Space Collaboration System) are developed and used as distance education systems between Japanese national universities. In the near future, a teacher's role will change from text based teaching to facilitating, advising, and consulting. His or her role will be more that of a designer of the learning environment. Therefore, a teacher has to constantly acquire new knowledge and methodologies. We have to build a free and flexible self-teaching environment for them under the concept of "continuous education". At the same time, we need to build a collaborative communication environment to support mutual deep and effective understanding among teachers.

In this paper, we propose a Distance Educational Model, which is based on the concept of School Based Curriculum Development and Training System, advocated by UNESCO and OECD/CERI (Center for Educational Research and Innovation). We describe the structure, function, mechanism and, finally, the educational meaning of this model. It is necessary to construct an individual, as well as a collaborative, learning environment that supports teachers' self-learning and training, by using Internet distributed environments and multimedia technologies. A teacher can choose the most convenient learning media to learn the contents (subject units) that s/he desires.

2. DISTANCE EDUCATIONAL MODEL BASED ON SCOUTS

Until now, when a teacher wanted to take a class on "IT-education", s/he had usually to leave the classroom or school. However, it is now possible to learn various kinds of subject contents by building a virtual school on the Internet environment.

2.1 Distance Educational Model

Our Distance Educational Model is built on three dimensions. The first one is subject-contents, which represents what the teachers want to learn. The second one represents teaching knowledge and skills as well as evaluation methods of students' learning activities. From the third axis, a favourite learning media (form) can be chosen, *e.g.* VOD, CBR, etc. By selecting a position on each of the three axes, a certain cell is determined. A cell stands for a "script", which describes the instruction guidelines of the learning contents, the self-learning procedure, and so on. Figure 1 shows the structure of this model. A more detailed explanation of each axis follows.

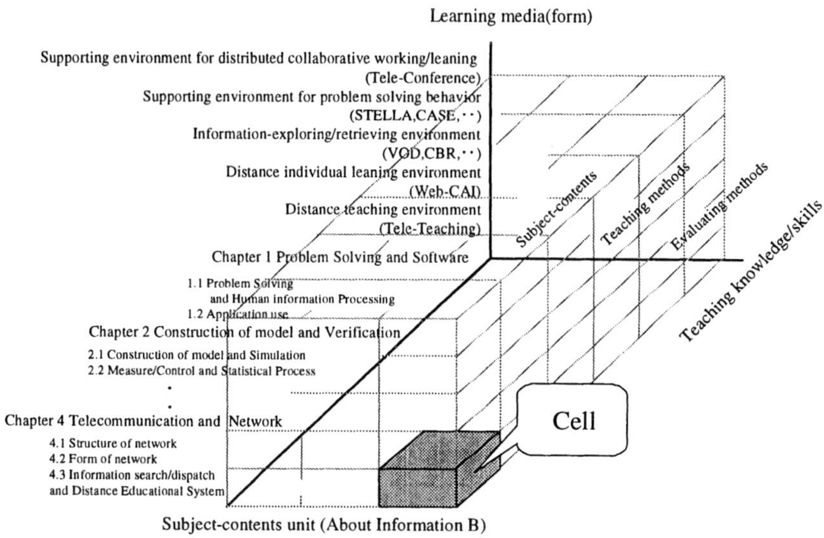

Figure 1. Structure of the Distance Educational Model

2.1.1 Subject-contents unit

In this study, we focus on the subject "Information", which is due to be established as a new obligatory subject in the regular courses of the academic high school system in Japan. The subject "Information" is composed of three sub-subjects, "Information A", "Information B" and "Information C". The contents of each sub-subject are as follows.

Information A: This sub-subject places importance on raising the fundamental skills and abilities to collect, process and transmit "information" using computers, the Internet and multimedia.

Information B: This sub-subject places importance on understanding the fundamental scientific aspects and the practical usage methods of "information".

Information C: This sub-subject places importance on fostering desirable and sound behaviour regarding participation, involvement and contribution in an information society. It focuses on understanding people's roles and the influence and impact of technology in the new information society.

2.1.2 Teaching knowledge/skills

On this dimension, we have represented three items, which are: sub-subject contents, teaching methods and evaluating methods for "information" classroom teaching. The item 'teaching methods' stands for how to use and apply IT, in order to enhance a student's problem solving ability. This involves comprehensive learning activities, such as problem recognition, investigation and analysis, planning and design, implementation and execution, evaluation, report and presentation. We aim at teachers acquiring the proper respective evaluation skills of students' achievements, for each of the above activities.

2.1.3 Learning media (form)

This dimension represents five different learning environments: (1) "Distance teaching environment (Tele-Teaching)", based on one-to-multi-sites telecommunications; (2) "Distance individual learning environment (Web-CAI)", based on CAI (Computer Assisted Instruction) using World Wide Web facilities; (3) "Information-exploring and retrieving environment", using VOD (Video on Demand) or CBR (Case Based Reasoning); (4) "Supporting environment for problem solving", by providing various effective learning tools; and (5) "Supporting environment for distributed collaborative working/learning", based on multi-multi-sites telecommunications. Brief explanations for each environment follow.

1. *Distance teaching environment (Tele-Teaching)*: This environment delivers the instructor's lecture image and voice information through the Internet, by using the real-time information dispatching function via VOD (Video On Demand).
2. *Distance individual learning environment (Web-CAI)*: This environment provides CAI (Computer Assisted Instruction) courseware with World Wide Web facilities on the Internet.
3. *Information-exploring and retrieving environment*: This environment delivers, according to the teacher's demand, the instructor's lecture image and voice information, which was previously stored on the VOD server. For delivery, the function 'dispatching information accumulated on the VOD server' is used. In addition, this environment provides a CBR system with short movies about classroom teaching practices.

4. *Supporting environment for problem solving*: This environment provides a tool library for performance support based on CAD Modelling tools, Spreadsheets, Authoring tools, and so on.
5. *Supporting environment for distributed collaborative working and learning*: This environment provides a groupware with a shared memory window, using text, voice and image information for trainees.

2.2 "Cell" definition

The concept of a "cell" in the Distance Educational Model is quite important because it generates the training scenario, including information to satisfy the teacher's needs, the subject materials learning-flow and the guidelines for self-learning navigation. The frame representation of the "cell" is shown in Table 1. These slots are used when the system guides the process of the teacher's self-learning.

Table 1. The frame representation of the "cell"

Frame-name:		
		Slot-value
Slot-name	Learning objectives for a student	Subjects which should be understood Subjects which should be mastered
	Subject-contents	The unit topic
	Teaching method	The students' supervision method and instructional strategies
	Evaluating method	The students' evaluation method
	Useful tools	The software used for the training activity
	Operational manual of tools	The software operation method used for the training activity
	Prepared media	The learning media which can be selected
	Guide script	The file which specifies the dialog between the trainee and the system

3. OUTLINE OF THE TEACHER TRAINING SYSTEM

The system configuration of the teacher's training environment is composed of two subsystems based on the Distance Educational Model. One of the subsystems is the training system, where a trainee can select and learn the subject s/he needs, guided by the script in the "cell". The other subsystem is an authoring system with creating and editing functions for "cell" description. The users of the second environment are, for example, IT-coordinators or IT-consultants, who can design lecture-plans in this environment.

3.1 Training system

The training system aims to support teachers' self-training. The configuration of this system is shown in Figure 2. The role of this system is first to identify a "cell" in the model, according to the teachers' needs. Then, the system tries to set up an effective learning environment, by retrieving the proper materials for the teacher, along with the "guide script" defined in the corresponding "cell". Therefore, the system offers programs for both Retrieving and Interpreting. The training system works thus:

STEP 1: Record the teacher's needs.
STEP 2: Select a "cell" in the Distance Education Model according to the teacher's needs.
STEP 3: Interpret the "cell" in the guide WM (Working Memory).
STEP 4: Develop the interactive training with the teacher according to the "guide script" in the guide WM.
STEP 5: Store the log-data of the dialog. The log-data collects information on the learning histories and teachers' needs and behaviours.
STEP 6: Provide the necessary and useful applications for the user's learning activities and set up an effective training environment.
STEP 7: Give guidance-information, according to the "cell" script guidelines, and decide on the proper "cell" for the next learning step.

Here, it is necessary to explain the dialog mechanism (algorithm) between user and system. The interpreter controls and develops the dialog process between user and machine according to the information defined in our "guide script" description language. This "guide script" description language (GSDL) consists of some tags and a simple grammar for interpreting a document, similar to the HTML (Hypertext Mark-up Language) on the World Wide Web.

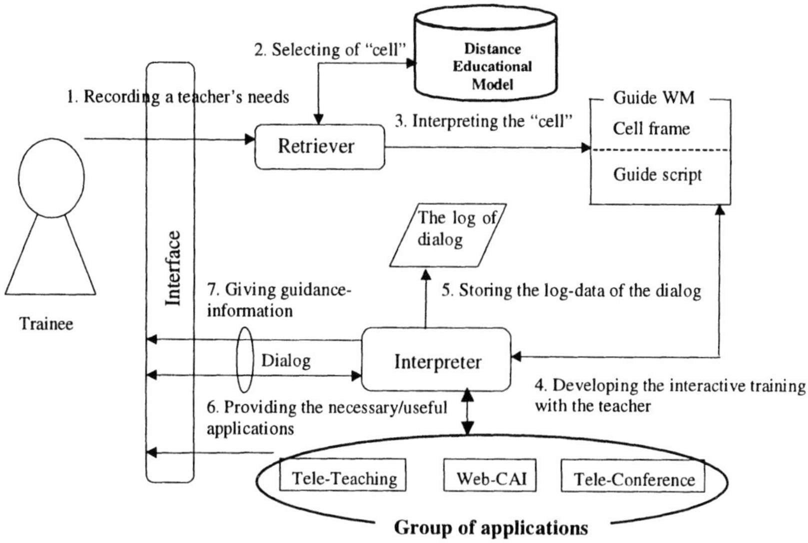

Figure 2. Configuration of training system

The interpreter understands the meanings of the tags, and interprets the contents. An example of GSDL is shown below.

1. **<free>** Definition: description of the text (instruction)
2. **<slot (num.)>** Definition: a link to a slot value in the "cell"
3. **<question>** Definition: questions to a trainee
4. **<choice>** Definition: branching control according to a trainee's response
5. **<exe>** Call: to relevant "cells"
6. **<app>** Definition: applications used for training activities (*e.g.* Tele-Teaching, etc.)

3.2 Authoring system for creating and editing a "cell" description

The system provides an authoring module to create and edit the information in the "cell". This module also offers the function of adding new "cells", in order to allow supervisors (experienced teachers) to design the teachers' training program. The configuration of this system is shown in Figure 3. The tasks that can be performed by this system are: adding new "cells", editing the existing "cells", receiving calls for Tele-Teaching lectures, and managing the lectures schedule. This system is composed of the "cell" frame creating module, and the "guide script" creating module. A cell design can be performed as shown in the following.

STEP 1: Get the slot-values of "student's learning objectives", "subject-contents/teaching method/evaluating method", and "useful tools" from the "cell".
STEP 2: Substitute the return value of the slot of the prepared media with the training-contents corresponding to the user's needs.
STEP 3: Substitute the slot-value in the "cell" for the corresponding tag in the "guide script" template.
STEP 4: If "Tele-Teaching" as learning media is selected, then get some information about the lecture, by referring the lecture-DB and the VOD short movie-DB.
STEP 5: Add the new "cell" to the Distance Educational Model.

The lecture-database consists of "lesson managing files" containing user-profile data, lecture schedules, trainees' learning records, lecture abstracts, and so on. The "guide script" template file contains tag-information, written in the "guide script" description language (GSDL), for all subject-contents items in the Distance Educational Model.

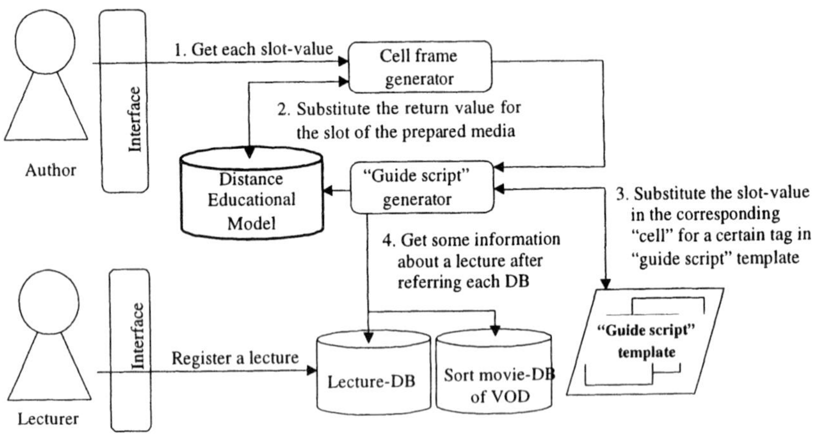

Figure 3. The procedure of "cell" description for creating/editing the authoring system

4. CONCLUSION

This paper proposed the Distance Educational Model called the "School Based Curriculum Development and Training System" (SCOUTS). This model stands for the networked virtual leaning environment based on a three dimensional representation, which has on the axes, (1) subject-contents, *e.g.*

"information" for the training, (2) teaching knowledge, skills and evaluation methods, and (3) learning and teaching media (forms). This represents a new framework for teachers' education in the coming networked age. We have mentioned the rationale of our system and explained the architecture of the training system via a 3D-representation model. Furthermore, we have described a "guide script" language. The aim of our system is to support teachers' self-learning, provided as in-service training. At the same time, we need to build rich databases by accumulating various kinds of teaching expertise. In such a way, the concept of "knowledge-sharing" and "knowledge-reusing" will be implemented. As a result, we trust that a new learning ecology scheme will emerge from our environment.

With this system, we can construct various kinds of learning forms and design interactive and collaborative activities among learners. Such an interactive learning environment can provide a modality of externalised knowledge-acquisition and knowledge-sharing, via the communication process, and support learning methods such as "Learning by asking", "Learning by showing", "Learning by Observing, "Learning by Exploring" and "Learning by Teaching/Explaining". Along with the learning effects expected from this system, we also aim at meta-cognition and distributed cognition, such as reflective thinking, self-monitoring, and so on. Therefore, we expect to build a new learning ecology, as mentioned above, through this system. Finally, we will apply this system to the real world and try to evaluate its effectiveness and usability from an experimental and practical point of view.

REFERENCES

Collis, B. (1999). Design, development and implementation of a WWW-based course-support system. *Proceedings of ICCE99, IOS Press.*

Nishinosono, H. (1998). A teacher education system for information education teachers at high school level in the information society. *Proceedings of the Conference JET.* Salvador, L.G. (1999). Continuing education through distance training. *Proceedings of ICCE99, IOS Press.*

Seki, K., Takaoka, R., Matsui, T., & Okamoto, T. (1998). A teaching model in distance education based on teacher's needs. *IEICE Technical Report, ET98-12.*

UNESCO. (1998). *World declaration on higher education for the twenty-first century: Vision and action.* Paris: UNESCO.

3

Educational Centres as Knowledge Organisations Training Future Knowledge Workers: The Role of IT

J. Osorio, C. Zárraga and J. Rodríguez
University of Las Palmas de Gran Canaria, E-35017 Las Palmas de Gran Canaria, Spain
Fax: +34 928 451829, E-mail: Osorio@empresariales.ulpgc.es

Key words: Information Technology, Knowledge Management, Education, ITEM Systems

Abstract: The main objective of this paper is to propose an IT related educational framework for centres which are responsible for future knowledge workers – primary schools, high schools, and universities. First, we analyse the latest changes in the business world due to the arrival of a new knowledge era. According to empirical and theoretical evidence, the first step necessary to succeed in knowledge management seems to be information technology (IT). After clarifying both the conceptual differences between information and knowledge, and the different knowledge types which are necessary to be managed, we analyse how IT can be a very useful tool for knowledge management in organisations. Second, we reflect upon the academic and social aims of educational centres, relating them to the inherent aims of knowledge based organisations. The goal is to try to integrate two perspectives that are not always easy to merge. As mentioned, the key point throughout this process can be IT, but it is necessary to train students of different levels in the basic skills, not only to accomplish the academic objectives, but also bearing in mind the role they are going to play in a more globally competitive environment. Finally, we consider the influence that these changes can have on educational centres, making them adapt to the environment by means of a learning attitude that allows them to become real knowledge centres. In this respect, information technology for educational management (ITEM) systems can play a vital role as catalysts for the process of change.

1. INTRODUCTION

The economy of every country is a direct reflection of its degree of business structure development. Corporations, the major employment creators, are under growing pressure from the increasingly competitive environment. Therefore, they have to continuously adapt and transform their business practices to survive. In this adaptive process, corporations are focusing their strategies more and more on the so-called intangible resources, fundamentally knowledge management and corporate learning. This trend has meant a dramatic change in traditional business management practices which were typically centred around physical assets.

This recent trend affects the training and skills that corporations now require from their present and future employees. Clerical and non-clerical workers are becoming knowledge workers and an important part of their job is to manage corporate knowledge appropriately. Consequently, educational centres of every level, as the main suppliers of qualified human resources, must rapidly adapt to the demands of the job market and give students the necessary skills to work successfully within corporations. The success of educational centres and, in many cases, their very survival, will depend on the compatibility of their students' training with the requirements of business corporations.

One key point in achieving this is the education and training given to students in information technology (IT) matters. Empirical evidence shows that the very first step necessary to succeed in knowledge management is to know and to master IT potential. Therefore it is necessary at every educational level – primary school, high school and university – to clearly identify the likely missions and functions of the respective graduates in the jobs in today's market place. Consequently, an important task for those responsible for education is to effectively plan the IT tools that students at each level must know and master.

Bearing in mind previous considerations, this paper attempts to propose an IT educational framework with the most suitable tools, objectives and training methodologies at each educational level. This framework must be adapted to the socially established general educational objectives and, at the same time, satisfy the demands of the business world in which most students will develop their professional activities in the future.

To achieve this goal it is also necessary to redefine the role of educational centres. Knowledge[1] is the most important resource that educational centres have in order to ensure that the output (students who have completed their education) are prepared for the functions that they will

[1] Not only the knowledge that they pass on to students, but, above all, the know-how to carry out the educational function in a more effective way.

perform in the future. In this process of knowledge acquisition, the centres become organisations that learn and the ITEM constitutes an important agent for learning, making a definitive contribution to defining this new role of educational centres.

The paper starts with an analysis of the latest changes in the business world due to the new knowledge era, which leads us to the conclusion that the knowledge management efforts of companies begin with the implementation of IT. Following this, we explain the role of IT in organisations whose competitive advantage is based on knowledge management using the hypertext style of organisational structure, as well as the new concept of heterarchy.

At this point, we review the social and academic aims of the educational system at the present time, which constitute the reference that must be taken into account. This is because companies' goals could cause conflict between their demands for employees' training and the socially settled objectives of the educacional system. However, it is important for the growth of joint attempts to closely integrate both sides – academic and economic – to improve the general performance at all levels, including the social one. Hence, knowing the business trend – that of companies relying on better knowledge management – and a potential way of integrating it with education aims by means of IT, we propose an educational framework for IT, trying to identify the computer skills that could be included in the formative curriculum of students according to their educational level.

To be able to put this educational framework into practice it is necessary to redefine the role of the educational centres. We consider a vision based on knowledge management to be necessary, and this is acquired after a process of continuous learning about how to teach or educate in a better way. With this purpose in mind, we reflect at the end of the paper that, in order to be successful, it is necessary to know how to take advantage of the potential offered by IT, and more specifically of the diverse tools that make up ITEM. By combining qualified human resources with the use of IT, the appropriate conditions for those changes required by the future environment can be created.

2. KNOWLEDGE AND INFORMATION TECHNOLOGY

Static theories of competition, associated with neoclassical microeconomics and the "structure-conduct-performance" school of industrial economics, are being displaced by the more dynamic approaches associated with the Austrian school of economics, especially with Schumpeter's concept of competition as a process of "creative destruction" (Schumpeter, 1934). This displacement has had profound implications for strategic management thinking and it has generated the resource-based view of the firm, which places more emphasis on the "supply-side" than the "demand side". This new strategic view has been closely associated with recent works on organisational capabilities, such as Prahalad and Hamel's work (1990), which argues that sustainable competitive advantage is dependent upon building and exploiting "core competences". These are capabilities which are fundamental to a firm's competitive advantage and which can be deployed across multiple product markets.

Indeed, competitive conditions in product markets are driven, in part, by the competitive conditions in resource markets. Thus, the speed with which positions of competitive advantage in product markets are undermined, depends upon the ability of challengers to acquire the resources needed to initiate a competitive offensive. Sustainability of competitive advantage, therefore, requires resources which are idiosyncratic (and therefore scarce), and not easily transferable or replicable. These criteria point to knowledge as the most strategically important resource which firms possess.

Many researchers have pointed out that for many firms their ability to create, share, and use knowledge will have a major impact on their future competitiveness; and some even state that the only sustainable competitive advantage in the future will be good or excellent organisational knowledge creation and good knowledge management (Toffler, 1990; Drucker, 1993; El Sawy *et al.*, 1997; Teece, 1998; Miles *et al.*, 1998). One hypothesis is that theories of organisational knowledge creation and a resource-based view can give new ideas on how to design and implant IT. Nowadays, there are two main reasons for the changing role of IT. First, there is a paradigm shift from information processing to knowledge creation. Second, the literature on knowledge management is to a large extent ignoring IT (Carlsson *et al.*, 1996).

On the other hand, from the empirical point of view, studies such as that conducted in 1997 by the Ernst & Young Center for Business Innovation, whose objective was to describe what firms are doing in order to manage knowledge and what else they think could be or should be done, show that 22% of the 431 US and European organisations studied think that restrictions over IT are a hindrance to the transfer of knowledge. Furthermore, many companies are progressing along similar lines when their knowledge management efforts start with the implementation of a technological capability, although when respondents were asked whether their organisations' ability to compete based on knowledge depends more upon people, process or technology issues, their aggregate responses placed the emphasis heavily on people (50%), with the other two areas carrying equal secondary weight (25% each). So, there is evidence of the knowledge management efforts of companies, starting with the implementation of a technological capability, which allows them (at least in principle) to capture and share corporate know-how. Only after this capability exists do the firms realise how vital other factors are (Ruggles, 1998).

3. INFORMATION TECHNOLOGY: A TOOL FOR KNOWLEDGE MANAGEMENT

To explain the role of information technology in organisations whose competitive advantage is based on knowledge management, we use the hypertext style of organisational structure, defined by Nonaka and Takeuchi (1995), as well as the new concept of heterarchy *versus* the classical concept of hierarchy, as defined by Hedlund (1994). The heterarchy arises from: (1) the dispersal of knowledge and strategic action initiative to "lower levels"; (2) shifting bases of leadership and composition of teams; (3) the importance of lateral internal communication and integration through shared culture; and (4) change of roles at all levels of the corporation. Therefore, a business organisation should have a nonhierarchical, self-organising structure working in tandem with its formal hierarchical structure. The most appropriate metaphor for such a structure comes from a "hypertext", which was originally developed in computer science. A hypertext organisational structure will have three layers: the business-system layer, the project-team layer, and the knowledge-base layer.

The central layer is the "business-system" layer, in which normal, routine operations are carried out. Since a bureaucratic structure is suitable for conducting routine work efficiently, this layer is shaped like a hierarchical pyramid, that is, this layer has a strong focus on vertical communication (Nonaka & Takeuchi, 1995). The IT community knows quite well how to design and implement systems for the business-system layer, mainly from an information processing perspective. Computer-based systems such as transaction processing systems, accounting information systems, and management information systems are good examples of this type of system (Carlsson *et al.*, 1996).

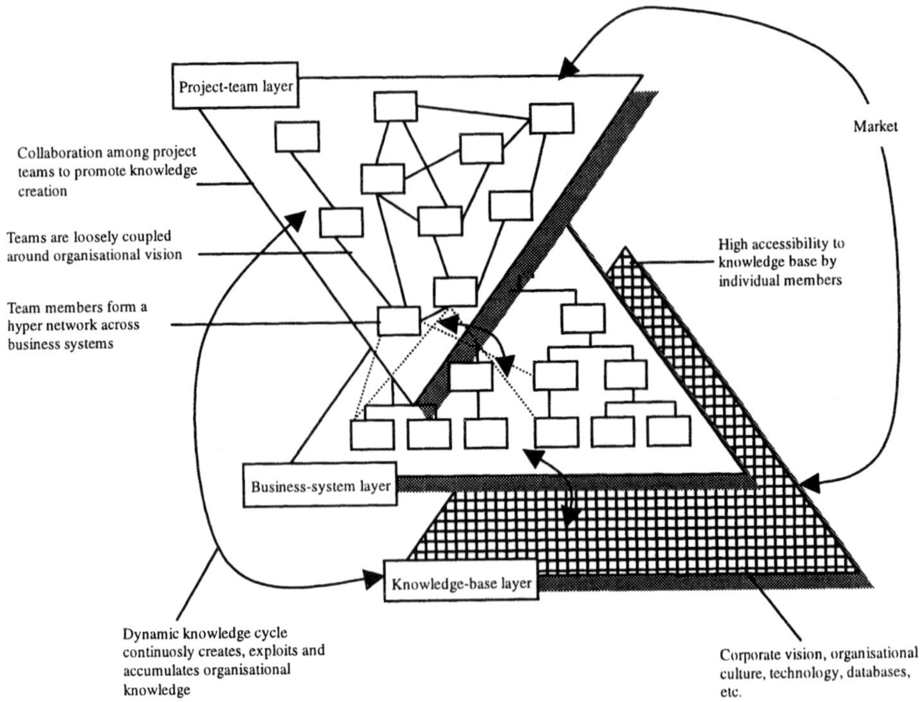

Figure 1. Hypertext organisation. Source: Nonaka and Konno (1993)

At the bottom is the "knowledge-base" layer, where organisational knowledge generated in the above two layers is recategorised and recontextualised in accordance with the firm's corporate vision, organisational culture, and technology. Corporate vision provides the direction in which the company should develop its technology or products, and clarifies the "field" in which it wants to play. Organisational culture directs the mindset and action of every employee. Technology helps to make knowledge accessible to the whole organisation (Nonaka & Takeuchi, 1995). For this, the key is that everybody in the organisation is aware of who knows what, who can help with what or who can use new information (von Hippel, 1988; Carlsson *et al.*, 1998). Information technology, as data warehousing or knowledge repositories and decision support tools, can make it possible for an organisation to store and to make accessible "what we know" as an organisation. Whatever the level of sophistication, repositories essentially compile data, information and knowledge through, and in the form of, processes that enable access throughout the company. In time, these repositories contribute to the maintenance of the firm's shared intelligence and organisational memory.

4. THE ROLE OF THE EDUCATIONAL SYSTEM

In the light of the described managerial reality, we believe that the educational system has to respond to the demand for qualified personnel coming from organisations whose competitiveness relies basically on knowledge management. Consequently, based on the theoretical and empirical evidence outlined previously, our objective centres on identifying what is the IT that, while fostering the specific objectives of educational centres (we can refer to them as the 'supply'), also prepares the students appropriately for their future incorporation into the companies (consequently the 'demand').

It can be stated that the existence of educational systems is a reality for all civilisations and, over the course of time, they have evolved, thus changing their pedagogic objectives. At the present time, almost every country belonging to the OECD designs its educational system in order to (Gairín, 1992):

- Boost the critical capacity;
- Provide knowledge;
- Develop the values of respect, autonomy and responsibility;
- Favour the processes of collaboration;
- Assist the diversity;
- Encourage the integration process; and
- Cultivate democratic values.

It is important to remember that the accomplishment of these pedagogic goals can be extremely difficult when the importance of the specific demands coming directly from the business system is not perceived. We refer here to the *glass bubble* syndrome, which means that educators are, on occasion, out of touch with the social and professional reality in which their present students will perform their work in the future. We believe that it is necessary for educational professionals, both academic and management staff, to be aware of the professional demands coming from the companies. As a first step, it might be useful to consider the educational centre itself as a knowledge management centre, in which the objective should be to reach excellence, promoting a better and more efficient spread and management of knowledge. This way, in the educational centres themselves, they would appreciate the importance of suitable teaching and application of the tools, including IT, that can contribute to the attainment of this goal, so stimulating feedback processes and a continuous improvement starting from the educational centres' own experience. The implications that the latter can have for ITEM systems may be crucial in facing the future.

Now centring on our objective, before proceeding to the identification of how IT can improve not only the goals of educational centres but also the market-specific training of future employees, it is worth identifying three different areas in the IT field: hardware, software and telecommunications. With reference to the first, hardware, we can now state that the personal computer (PC) constitutes the present, and most likely future, standard platform, due, among other reasons, to its growing power, integration capacity, and ease of use as well as its low cost. Companies tend to focus their information management processes around PCs, thus abandoning technological formulas which not long ago constituted the *de facto* standard. On the other hand, insofar as telecommunications is concerned, it can to be said that the TCP/IP protocol has become the basis which has allowed the dramatic development of communications in recent years. It is foreseeable that in the next few years computers will work exclusively on this protocol in any type of communication, both internal and external to the organisation.

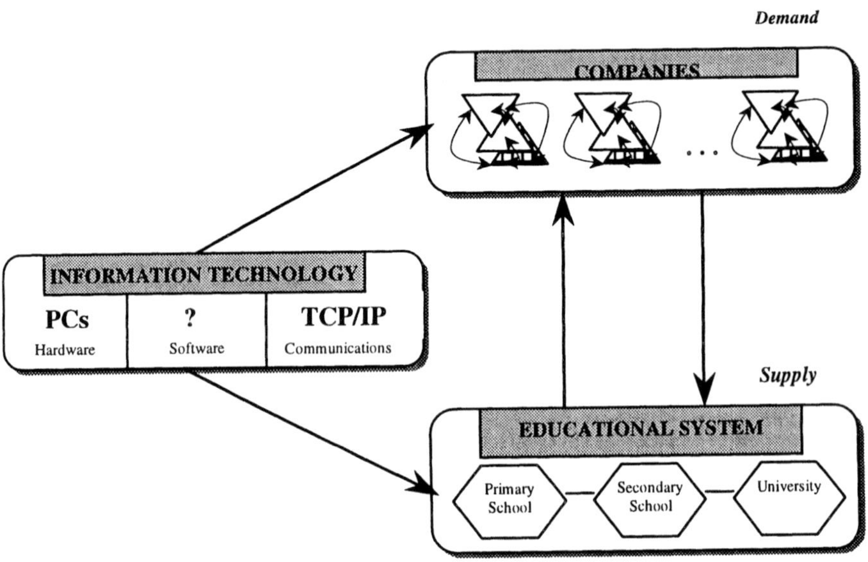

Figure 2. IT educational framework

It is not so easy, however, to identify optimal technological solutions in the software field. The wide range of computer applications and software developers produces some confusion when trying to identify the tools that should be incorporated as a fundamental part of students' education. Nevertheless, we believe that bearing in mind the personnel needs of companies on the one hand and the pedagogic objectives established by the educational system on the other, and with the added advantage of knowing what will probably be the standard in hardware and telecommunications, we can outline which software applications should be incorporated into the educational curriculum. At this point it would be appropriate to differenciate between educational levels according to the specific objectives associated with each educational stage. In summary, the IT educational framework now taking shape is represented in Figure 2, where the companies that nowadays base their competitiveness on knowledge management interact with the current educational system, IT being the fundamental nexus among them.

5. AN EDUCATIONAL FRAMEWORK FOR IT

Bearing in mind the considerations previously outlined, we will now attempt to define more precisely what the software tools should be, and to what end they should be included in the formative curriculum of students according to their educational level. It is important not to forget that when teaching software it is necessary to make an effort to concentrate on the basic and stable principles; those always remain, independent of the developer and the version of the computer application. This way it can be assured that the student is prepared to adapt to any format change that might be carried out on the tool.

Primary education (approximately 6-12 years). Although the specific educational objectives vary according to country and culture, it can be said that the main objective at this level consists of instilling in the students a base of academic knowledge and social attitudes that allow them to adapt to their social environment. The use of computers as a complement to classes, helping students to learn by means of educational games and tutorials, can also notably contribute to their familiarisation with a tool that will accompany them throughout their professional lives. Once the basics of the tool (the PC) are known to the students, it is worth letting them know the potential offered by the Internet, albeit always closely monitored by the teacher. Showing the existence of other cultures, promoting communication with students in other parts of the world, as well as teaching the possibility of accessing knowledge through the Internet permits attainment of both educational and social objectives at the same time at this educational level.

Secondary education (approximately 12-18 years). Two main groups of students can be distinguished: on the one hand, the students that join the professional world on concluding this educational level and, on the other hand, the students that stay in the educational system to continue with university careers. Regarding the first group, companies usually employ personnel with secondary studies fundamentally to work in operational activities. Companies expect employees at this level to have enough knowledge and social skills to successfully integrate into their workforce. School-leavers are expected to be familiar with the operation of productivity tools, such as word processors, spreadsheets and databases. Companies that base their competitiveness on knowledge also require employees with sufficient ability to contribute, by means of IT, to the improvement of products and services, adding value in the process and increasing the quality offered to clients. Students that stay in the educational system to continue with university careers, should also know the productivity tools in order to use them during their future studies.

It can be gathered from the above that at this level it is necessary to teach the productivity tools, but with the basic difference that this teaching places emphasis on the students' ability to model problems by means of the computer. The objective is to teach students to be not mere users of software applications, but rather to know how to create simulation and optimisation models. Finally, from the point of view of the development of collaboration attitudes, it is important at this level to encourage collaborative work, both internally in the class by means of groupware tools on a local area network (LAN), and externally by means of groupware tools on the World Wide Web (WWW). If students begin to use this type of tool at this level, the likelihood of its continued use in the university or in the company increases, thus promoting a desirable attitude in all students and workers.

University education. At this level there are a wide range of professional careers available. Graduate students are mostly recruited to middle or top management positions in a company. They are expected to have socio-technical capabilities, the capacity for middle and long-term planning, and problem solving abilities. Knowledge management based companies also expect this grade of employee to be able to instill in the rest of the organisation the importance of the practices of knowledge management as well as to be pioneers in the use of tools that facilitate this objective. On the other hand, nowadays IT is, as has been formerly shown, the first step towards the operationalisation of knowledge management in companies. Therefore, the university student should know the whole range of possibilities offered by professionally related software applications at any given moment, as well as having the capacity to know, to distinguish and to assimilate the new tools that are continually being launched.

At university level it should be assumed that students manage the productivity tools with ease, and that the use of the Internet as a means of acquiring knowledge and of group collaboration is second nature. Depending on the degree chosen, the students should be trained in the use of specific tools with potential for their professional careers, but always stressing the underlying models of the tool and not incidental matters like operational handling. The emphasis should be centred on expert systems (ES), decision support systems (DSS) and executive information systems (EIS). These tools will vary continually throughout the professional career of the knowledge worker, but he/she will have sufficient skills to adapt to the new challenges that their use implies *vis-a-vis* the objectives specified by the knowledge management based companies.

All the above-mentioned has, logically, important implications for educational centres in their potential new role of knowledge management centres. In short, these do function as such and their academic and management staff must be those responsible for achieving this. Information and its more effective use may be the key to educational centres, just like companies, reaching better performance levels. The mentioned software tools, in the hands of the academic and management staff, also constitute ITEM systems, one advantage of which is that "[the ITEM systems] provide more time for pupil contact, thus enhancing interaction, positive intervention, feedback and discussion with implications for a more collaborative learning environment" (Visscher & Wild, 1997:271).

6. A NEW VISION FOR EDUCATIONAL CENTRES

Facing the challenges of the future and the demands arising from labour markets, educational centres should be aware of and react to the need to become centres of excellence. This is important if they want to offer society competent graduates and also attract new students who, with the proliferation of public and private, attendance-learning and distance-learning centres, will have more choice of study locations. For this reason, educational centres should take advantage of their resources and differential capabilities, exploiting their strengths and trying to reduce or eliminate their weaknesses.

Of all the resources of an organisation, the most important is knowledge, because it is the most difficult to transfer and replicate. Knowledge is generated in an individual way, and in our case the education system puts at each teacher's disposal the means to increase his or her individual knowledge. However, it is the responsibility of the centre to apply existing knowledge in the improvement of the educational process. The logic is to incorporate the knowledge of many performers (the teachers) efficiently and to promote the means that lead to an increased level of shared knowledge among the members of the centre. To attain this objective it is necessary to make the centre's members aware of the need to incorporate continuous learning into the day-to-day culture, thus transforming the workplace into what is called a learning organisation.

The learning process is long and continuous since organisations learn while they carry out their activities. This leads to an increase in the degree of knowledge and is translated into the capacity to achieve the desired results and to transform a centre into one of excellence. Furthermore, a series of abilities should be acquired within a set of activities, which include: (1) the systematic resolution of problems; (2) experimenting with new approaches to teaching; (3) learning from the experiences and better practices of other educational centres; and (4) the fast and efficient transfer of knowledge throughout the entire organisation (Garvin, 1993). Therefore, the challenge consists of making effective use of IT in order to contribute to the educational management of centres while understanding that it should also embrace the administration of knowledge, in other words, favouring the communication of individual knowledge among teaching staff so that it becomes a shared asset.

7. CONCLUSIONS

The relationship between the offer and the demand, as established by the neoclassic economists, is widely accepted to explain the operation of the market place. In a similar way, we can accept that an offer and demand relationship exists between educational centres and companies. A mutual and constant adaptation that has a bearing on the improvement of society and the economy is necessary. Companies are under numerous changes and pressures, one of which is the need to identify and appropriately manage the knowledge existent within them. IT is the basic instrument for managing this knowledge and requires qualified workers who know how to obtain the greatest possible benefit from it. The challenge for educational centres lies in learning how to incorporate the teaching of IT with that objective in mind, but it implies that they themselves also have to become knowledge management organisations.

It is true to say that, for many years, primary schools, secondary schoools and universities have incorporated IT courses into their programmes, and also that this has been a consequence of trying to adapt to social and economic changes. Most of the IT tools mentioned above are already taught at educational centres, but an in-depth analysis would show the merely instrumental nature that they are given. This is very similar to what happened in language teaching in non-English speaking countries some decades ago: English was taught and learnt as a complementary subject without stressing its imminent importance in a more global world where it was going to be necessary to master a common language. Continuing with the comparison, nowadays IT teaching seems like the mere acquisition of skills for using a computer package without showing their importance as potential knowledge vehicles from very early on in a child's life. The increase in use of IT in organisations in the near future is foreseeable as the importance of knowledge management becomes more and more recognised. Therefore, the point should be to change the perspective or philosophy while teaching IT in educational centres. That could have great impact on the educational culture, with some enthusiastically supporting it, and others reacting against it.

We consider that our view of a different philosophy when teaching IT in educational centres could promote discussion and consequently give rise to various implications for them. The first we have identified as the pressure on educational centres to become real knowledge management centres, thus constituting an asset for ensuring the quality of their output. In this way, we believe that ITEM systems can be crucial in this challenge. IT not only has to be taught, thinking of future knowledge workers, but it has also to be applied to make the centre itself a knowledge management based organisation. The latter gives rise to a new dimension for ITEM systems that justifies their importance and highlights the need to further research this area.

REFERENCES

Brown, J.S., & Duguid, P. (1998). Organizing knowledge. *California Management Review, 40* (3), 90-111.

Carlsson, S.A., El Sawy, O.A., Eriksson, I., & Raven, A. (1996). Gaining competitive advantage through shared knowledge creation: In search of a new design theory for strategic information systems. *Proceedings of the 4th European Conference on Information Systems*. Lisbon, Portugal, 2-4 July, 1996.

Cash, J.L., McFarlan, F.W., McKenney, J.L., & Applegate, L.M. (1992). *Corporate information systems management* (3rd ed.). Boston, MA: Irwin.

Drucker, P.F. (1993). *Post-capitalist society*. Oxford: Butterworth Heinemann.

El Sawy, O.A., Eriksson, I., Carlsson, S.A., & Raven, A. (1997). *Shared knowledge creation spaces around the new product development process*. Working Paper, University of Southern California.

Gairín, J. (1992). El proyecto curricular en el marco de una escuela renovada. In *Orientaciones teórico-prácticas para la elaboración de proyectos curriculares*. Madrid: Ministerio de Educación y Ciencia.

Garvin, D.A. (1993). Building a learning organization. *Harvard Business Review, 71* (4), 78-91.

Hedlund, G. (1994). A model of knowledge management and the N-form corporation. *Strategic Management Journal, 15,* 73-90.

Hippel, E. von, (1988). *The sources of innovation.* New York: Oxford University Press.

Miles, G., Miles, R.E., Perrone, V., & Edvinsson, L. (1998). Some conceptual and research barriers to the utilization of knowledge. *California Management Review, 40* (3), 281-288.

Nonaka, I., & Konno, N. (1998). The concept of *Ba. California Management Review, 40* (3), 40-54.

Nonaka, I., & Takeuchi, H. (1995). *The knowledge-creating company.* New Yord: Oxford University Press.

Prahalad, C., & Hamel, G. (1990). The core competence of the corporation. *Harvard Business Review, 68* (3), 79-111.

Ruggles, R. (1998). The state of the notion: Knowledge management in practice. *California Management Review, 40* (3), 81-89.

Schumpeter, J.A. (1934). *The theory of economic development.* Cambridge, MA: Harvard University Press.

Teece, D. (1998). Capturing value from knowledge assets: The new economy, markets for know how, and intangible assets. *California Management Review, 40* (3), 55-79.

The Ernst & Young Center for Business Innovation and Business Intelligence (1997). *Twenty questions on knowledge in the organization.* Ernst & Young. http://www.businessinnovation.ey.com/research/knowle/survey/survey.html.

Toffler, A. (1990). *Powershift: Knowledge, wealth and violence at the edge of the 21st century.* New York: Bantam Books.

Visscher, A., & Wild, P. (1997). The potential of information technology in support of teachers and educational managers managing their work environment. *Education and Information Technologies, 2* (4), 263-274.

Developing Software for School Administration and Management

Incorporating Flexibility

M. Bajec, M. Krisper and R. Rupnik
University of Ljubljana, Faculty of Computer & Information Science, Trzaska 25, 1000 Ljubljana,Slovenia
e-mail: marko.bajec@fri.uni-lj.si

Key words: Software Flexibility, Business Rules Technologies

Abstract: Flexibility is one of the most important characteristics of software systems for computerised school management and administration, in particular if the software has to be used in several institutions. Given that school institutions are diverse in many aspects and have their own specific needs, several problems are faced when developing unified software. In this paper we describe an approach to information system planning and development, which we believe can help to gain the required software flexibility. The main purpose of the paper is not to examine technical issues on information technologies but to emphasise the possibilities that have to be considered when developing software in support of management and administration in schools.

1. INTRODUCTION

Studies on the use of Computerised Information Systems in schools have proved the correlation between the existing variance in the type and extent of School Information System usage and the ability to adapt software to institution-specific needs (Mahnic, 1997; Wild & Fung, 1996). Flexibility is an example of a software characteristic that makes transition to new software smoother and easier. Of course, there are several other indispensable features that can affect the decision whether or not to use or adapt the system. In our opinion, system developers have to be aware of all the requirements in order to develop adequate systems. Business users, in our case school managers, also have to be aware of the possibilities offered by contemporary technologies and approaches in information system development. A few years ago it would not have been expected that a system would be able to take instructions only by voice, without using a keyboard or mouse – this was simply not possible. New technologies, however, made this dream a reality.

We will use this opportunity, therefore, to introduce a rather unknown approach to information system development. Since our domain is information science, and we have some experience in planning and developing software for school administration and management (Rupnik *et al.*, 1997; Mahnic, 1997), we believe that school management and administration is a good example of an application domain that can fit several modern development concepts. One of these is a Business Rules Approach that primarily focuses on software flexibility issues.

2. WHY FLEXIBILITY?

The need for new approaches and technologies emerged from the problems that we experienced with the development of an information system for higher-education institutions in Slovenia (Rupnik *et al.*, 1997) and later with the system maintenance. The project was funded by the Ministry of Education and Sport and took place at the beginning of 1995. The objective was to develop an information system that supports centralised processing of enrolment applications, which is a common process for all Slovenian universities and independent colleges. As there were many institutions (with many different study programmes), each of which had followed its own enrolment policies and rules, we had a tremendously difficult job developing a rigorous, and at the same time flexible, enrolment policy model. Even today, five years from the launch of the Enrolment System, we still have to make changes required by faculty management.

Similar findings were discovered when developing a students records information system (Mahnic & Vilfan, 1995) for the University of Ljubljana, the largest university in Slovenia. It has 26 member institutions (twenty faculties, three academies and three colleges), more than 40,000 students, over 2,600 teaching and research personnel, and an administrative staff of about 1,250. The purpose of the development project was to support entrance examinations, enrolment, examination records, alumni records, various analyses and statistical surveys. All the applications were written in co-operation between the Faculty of Computer and Information Science and the University Computing Centre, with the support of the European Union

Tempus program (project IEP 1852 "Computerisation of Administration and Management in Higher Education", 1991-94). As Mahnic (1997) states, in Slovenia faculties have substantial autonomy within their universities, and they often have their own policy regarding the use of information technology. Thus the development of an integrated university information system was not only a difficult technical task, but required a substantial organisational effort. Among the other findings discovered through close examination of the experiences of other institutions and initiatives in foreign countries (McDonough, 1992; Powell, 1991; Frackmann, 1991, 1992; Schutte, 1991), was that the system has to offer a certain level of flexibility in order to handle all the differences among the member institutions (in organisation, administration, etc.). Even though some specific solutions required by particular institutions were not a part of an overall agreement, the project team was forced to consider them in order to retain user satisfaction. Again, the question was, how to achieve the required level of flexibility?

2.1 Business Rules and Flexibility

Recently, much effort has been put into developing applications that are flexible and easier to change and adapt. Unfortunately, most of today's applications do not apply to these characteristics, as changes require the modification of low-level program code. Of course, not all changes are equally difficult. If a customer wants to have an additional dialogue box incorporated into the user interface, we can (usually) do that without any substantial effort. But what if, for example, a process of entrance examinations has been changed due to some additional rules that have been put into operation? Or what if a current system allows a student to select four course offerings for the coming semester, but now management would like to allow students to select four course offerings plus two alternative choices, in case the student cannot be assigned to a primary selection? From an organisational point of view, these changes are rather trivial, but in terms of a software change, they are difficult and time consuming. In fact, this is commonly the case: the rules change constantly at a policy level, while we cannot keep up with the software that is used to implement them.

These kinds of rules are known as "Business Rules". Although the name is rather confusing[1], it has become a widely accepted term within information science. Since there is no common definition that would clearly explain the concept of a business rule, various inconsistencies can be noticed

[1] The adjective "business" only causes confusion, as it forces us to think that business rules can apply to the development of business applications only. In fact, they apply to all kinds of applications.

when reading papers on business rules or using tools that claim to support them. For the purposes of this paper, a business rule will represent a statement that defines or constrains some aspect of the organisation's behaviour. Here are some examples:

- A candidate can apply to a maximum of three study programmes at the same or different institutions.
- Each study programme is composed of several courses.
- A date must be specified for an examination and cannot be changed after it has been published.
- A student must register for an exam at least three workdays before the examination date. After that, any registration is rejected.
- If a candidate is not a full-time student, her/his registration to an exam is automatically cancelled, unless she/he has preliminarily paid for the examination.
- If a student has failed an examination more than three times, the board of examiners must be convened. In addition, the student must pay for the examination.

According to various discussions (GUIDE, 1995; Barnes & Kelly, 1997; Ross, 1997; Hurwitz, 1997), business rules have a significant impact on software flexibility and scalability. If not presented properly, for instance if buried in the program code, they can be very difficult to manage and maintain. The most common problems that arise as a result are:

- Every change of business rules requires programming.
- Business rules are distributed across the application logic; thus the place where the change has to be made is hard to find.
- Business rules are dependent and interrelated chunks of logic. Therefore they have to be modified carefully, considering the possible effect on the other rules.
- It is very difficult to control business rules, as there is no common place where they are stored.
- Since the need for changes to rules usually arises from organisation requirements with which developers are not necessarily familiar, there is a risk the requirements will be misunderstood.

These are only a few of the problems that stimulated the development of a new strategy that is primarily focused on business rules. The main idea of this approach is to conceptually, logically and physically separate business rules from the other parts of application, data and functionality, while making them easy to access, view, modify and manage. Achieving those goals results in improved application flexibility and scalability.

Before discussing the concept of a business rules approach and its associated technologies, we will first examine how the rules are managed within the traditional application development life cycle and traditional applications.

3. TRADITIONAL APPROACHES TO FLEXIBILITY AND ADAPTABILITY

In order to make applications adaptable and flexible, developers have been using several different approaches for a long time. The most common traditional methods include parameterisation and using database mechanisms.

3.1 Parameterisation

One method of adding flexibility and adaptability to an application is to parameterise the application and its components. These parameters may be then set in a configuration file or in a database, and can be managed through a configuration utility. In doing so, the application can be adapted to different environments and situations just by parameter settings, without any programming effort.

The parameterisation technique proves useful when used to provide parameters for the business rules. Although the business rules remain hidden in the application logic, they can be modified through parameters, without any need for changing the program code. In addition, end users can make business rules modifications, if they are provided with simple and user-friendly configuration utilities.

However, this approach presupposes that the development team can foresee all kinds of changes that are likely to be required. Moreover, it presupposes that the development team able to programme and parameterise all additional cases. This requires the parameterisation of all logical decisions (decision logic has to be used or bypassed, and the variables used have to be stored as modifiable parameters). Consequently, this is an extreme burden on the application developer. In addition, application testing suffers from a combinatorial explosion effect that sometimes requires an additional application in order to configure the parameters correctly. These parameters themselves will often be interrelated, requiring assumptions and rules to be encoded in the parameter-modifying application, with similar problems.

3.2 Using Database Mechanisms

Most applications rely to a greater or lesser extent on a persistent data store that is usually based on relational database technology. Relational Database Management Systems (RDBMS) provide the so-called "triggers" that have the ability to execute actions immediately before or after particular events occur. This is when a record is inserted into a database, when a record is modified, and when a record is deleted from the database. Actions executed by triggers are written in Structured Query Language (SQL) and are stored either as the trigger body, or as a database procedure.

Because of those attributes, both triggers and database procedures can be very useful to implement business rules. For example, by using a "before-insert" trigger the record can be checked (and refused if it violates any business rule) before it is actually inserted. Since the implementation of the business rules resides in the database itself, modifications are application independent and can be performed without accessing the application logic. The advantages of such an approach are as follows:

- The formal representation of business rules is based on the SQL language, which is close to natural language.
- As business rules remain stored in the database, they are independent of the application logic.
- Business rules are not dispersed over a number of clients – they are stored on the database server.
- Modifications of business rules can be performed remotely (remote accessibility is one of the most important features of database servers).
- The place where the particular business rules are implemented is easier to find, since we know the actions that initiate them.
- Adding a new business rule does not necessary require changes to the application code.

Of course, there are some disadvantages as well. First, the approach suffers from being data- and database-dependent. Second, it cannot easily provide rule support for client or middle-tier applications that deal with complex business objects and business processes. And finally, such an approach forces the data store to be a process engine, a task that database engines are not optimised for.

4. BUSINESS RULES APPROACH

Till now we have only discussed problems regarding the implementation and execution of rules. However, the shortcomings of the traditional development life cycle come from other phases as well. According to proponents of a business rules approach, there is no support in conventional development processes for business rules acquisition, modelling and design (Hurwitz, 1997). In their opinion, business rules should be represented as a distinct concept within application analysis, design and implementation, and should not be treated implicitly through other perspectives that primarily focus on information resources like data, functions, processes, etc.

The business rules approach therefore suggests additional activities to be carried out in support of business rules philosophy:

- Business rules discovery;
- Business rules classification;
- Information resource object mapping;
- Business rules implementation; and
- Business rules change management (dependency, efficiency, versioning, traceability).

From all the activities listed above, we will only focus on the implementation phase. As we mentioned at the beginning, our intention is only to emphasise the possibilities of modern technologies (the technologies that end users work with). The scope, of course, is software flexibility.

5. BUSINESS RULES ASSOCIATED TECHNOLOGIES

According to the findings of the GIGA Information Group (Rymer, 1997), business rules have begun to get appropriate attention as a modelling approach (Gottesdiener, 1997), as well as an important meta-element addressed by software development tools. It is expected that developers building event-driven relational database applications will be the largest market segment for business rules tools. Besides the fact that the major database vendors are targeting this opportunity (Rymer, 1997), the appearance of some new business-oriented development tools confirms these predictions. Considering the business rules representation, implementation and execution, these tools can be classified as follows (Barnes & Kelly, 1997):

- Database-independent tools;
- Server-based tools; or
- Rule-based systems.

5.1 Database-Independent Tools

Database-independent tools use database mechanisms to enforce business rules, which seems rather confusing at first. However, different from the typical RDBMS[2] that we mentioned in previous sections, these tools support codes for triggers and procedures to be created automatically, and managed within the tool. This effectively moves the creation and management of data-centred business rules up one level to an application development tool rather than a database-specific tool.

Development tools that are based on such an approach presuppose that business rules form sufficient information (together with other rules) for developing any business application of a classical type. Through interviews and business area analysis, the analysts begin to form structure for the data elements required by the end user. The analyst identifies tables, columns, data types, data relationships and other structure-based rules (data rules). Instead of requiring the end user to verify the data model, the tool creates components for the database and a window interface to review the structure by working with the application (based on those rules). If the application does not match the rules of the business, the analyst can immediately change the structure rules. The user-interface is then specified further by using implementation rules (presentation rules). Finally, the specification of all other business rules takes place. The tool usually provides interfaces to capture, describe, formalise, and implement business rules.

[2] RDBMS – Relational Database Management Systems.

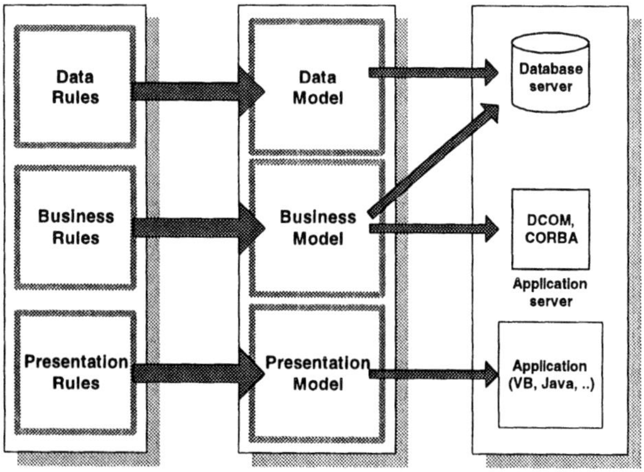

Figure 1. From rules to application

A good example of this type of product is Vision Software's *Vision Builder*[3], which automatically generates the appropriate stored procedures and triggers that reside in the target database.

The most important benefit of using such an approach to develop business applications is when the application needs to be changed and maintained. Because the complete information is stored in one place – in the repository – modifications can be easily made and the components can be automatically regenerated. However, this presupposes that the application is, and can be, 100% generated from the repository information. (The question of 100% generation goes beyond the scope of our discussion; it relies on sophisticated libraries and template sets of classical business applications modules.)

5.2 Server-Based Tools

Another way of ensuring business rules is to implement them as an application service. An example of a product associated with this type of approach is Usoft's *Developer*[4], which, like previous database-independent tools, assures that the application is automatically derived from the business rules (including implementation rules). The peculiarity here is that once the business rules are captured and stored in the repository, no further programming is required to fire and process those rules. The business rules processor does it all automatically. The tool also creates both the database

[3] Vision Software, http://www.vision-soft.com
[4] USOFT, Inc., http://www.usoft.com

and the other required components of three-tier architecture. Client-side applications then invoke objects, methods or functions on the server that contain business rules. Thus the main application and data-related logic reside on the application server and not in the database itself.

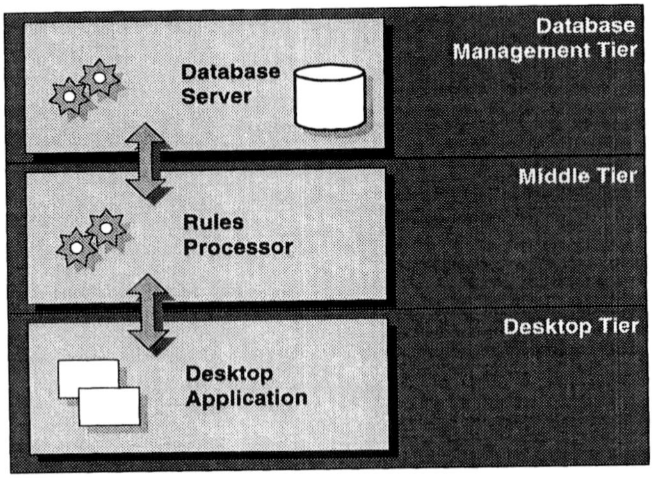

Figure 2. Rules processor: middle-tier service

Such an approach brings additional advantages. Developers do not need to worry about when the rules need to be fired and in what order they should be fired, because the rules processor handles all this. Another important advantage is technological independence. While the application architecture follows the three-tier architecture industry standard (known as ANSI/SPARC three-tier architecture), the different components of a business application remain independent. In this way, as better technologies are developed to implement the separate tiers, these new technologies can be "plugged in" to supersede less efficient methods.

5.3 Rule-Based Systems

All procedural languages are built upon the foundational concept of procedural flow, sometimes called the control flow. Programs written in languages like C, C++, Java, Basic, etc. are all based on control flow. The text of such programs is executed left to right, top to bottom, as the source code would be read. If we know the statement of procedural code being executed, we can always determine which statement will be executed next.

The benefits of procedural languages are predictability and straightforward mapping to today's serial, Von Neuman architectures, which make them very popular and commonly used program languages. However, their drawback is that they are difficult to use. The fact is that if we want our computer to compute something, we must first take all the specifications and constraints out of the problem and then organise them into a set of loops and conditional sentences that correctly describe how the computer should behave in the face of every problem it might encounter. This, of course, is not an easy job, otherwise there would be no shortage of software engineers, and maintenance costs would be probably much lower.

One example of a program language that follows to a rather different philosophy is a rule-based language. The most important characteristic that distinguishes it from the procedural language (beside the fact that there is no control flow in the rule-based language) is that with a rule-based architecture the system, not a software engineer, is responsible for mapping specifications and constraints into executable code. Unlike the procedural languages, rule-based languages take independent statements of if-then-else rules and automatically integrate their 'if' parts into a single, integrated and efficient conditional logic, which is directly executable by an inference engine. The inference engine is the core of every rule-based system. It monitors the applicability of the conditions of rules against a database. Whenever the database changes, whether by adding, deleting, or modifying a record in the database, all the rules are checked and fired if necessary.

Rule-based languages have been used for a long time, since they are the essence of every expert and knowledge-based system. They can be very useful if used as a language for specifying conditional or declarative knowledge. Moreover, they can be useful to specify business rules as they represent a special class of rules only. In fact, according to the findings of the GIGA Information Group (Rymer, 1997), "the interest in business rules will fuel expanded use of rule-based systems in commercial applications. Business rules products that are easily integrated with a variety of languages, platforms, and legacy systems will be the most successful." The ability of integration and coexistence is actually the essential difference between the so-called expert systems products of the 1980s and contemporary rules products. The classic rule-based system architecture is shown in Figure 3.

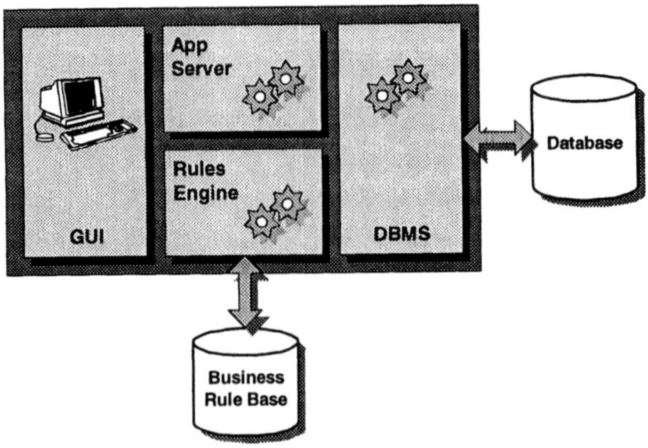

Figure 3. Rule-based system

Today's rules products can be easily integrated with different procedural program languages, various databases, and even with leading GUI tools. Neuron Data's *Elements Expert*[5] and ILOG's *Ilog Rules*[6] are good examples of such products.

There are many benefits of using rule-based systems instead of conventional development tools, when engineering systems for change. The most important are gathered below.

The key benefits of rule-based systems are (Barnes & Kelly, 1997):

- *Incremental development and rapid prototyping*. The rules can be run and tested the moment they are added to the system. Unlike traditional programming tools such as C++ or C, changes to the rules do not require recompilation, re-linking and re-deploying.
- *Understandable units of business practice*. Rules in the rule-base are self-contained chunks of logic, representing single concepts. This helps their readability and understandability.
- *No control flow*. Unlike a conventional program that usually has a single starting point and a set sequence of execution, there is no control flow in a rule-based approach. Rules can start to execute from any point in the rule-base.
- *Consistency*. In comparison to conventional code, incomplete, incorrect, irrelevant or redundant rules are much easier to find, since they stick out from the system.

[5] Neuron Data, Inc., http://www.neurondata.com
[6] ILOG Inc., http://www.ilog.com

- *Ability to work with incomplete and missing information.* In many business situations, it is not always possible to provide complete and verifiable data. Rule-based systems can deal with such cases of incomplete information – the rule engine is able to work with the special values "unknown" (not relevant in the case of a particular calculation) and "not-known" (the value is not known).

6. SUMMARY

The business rules approach that has been introduced in this paper follows a new philosophy that forces application developers to deal with business rules explicitly. The tools based on such an approach efficiently separate the business rules apart from the other applications components, describing them in both business and formal language. Even though there is no tool that would support the intuitive path leading from definition to implementation of business rules (Gottesdiener, 1997), we can get several advantages out of it.

End users of school information systems would find the business rules approach and related technologies very valuable. Programmers are able to:

- Develop applications that are easier to adapt to different environments;
- Involve end-users in application development;
- Let the end-user control the rules;
- Let the end-user maintain the rules; and
- Let the end-user simulate (test) different rule scenarios (how would the system behave if some rules are changed, added, removed, etc.).

Despite the fact that a business rules approach can be used in a variety of situations, it may not be applicable to all application domains. However, when engineering systems that have to offer a certain level of flexibility (and school information systems are a good example), such an approach is valuable.

REFERENCES

Barnes, M., & Kelly, D. (1997). Play by the rules. *Byte* (Special Report), *22* (6), 98-102.

Frackmann, E. (1991). Information for institutional administration and management in German higher education. *CRE-action*, *3*, 29-46.

Frackmann, E. (1992). HIS: The German initiative for administrative computing in higher education, Information for institutional administration and management in German higher education. *Higher Education Management*, *4* (3), 317-328.

Gottesdiener, E. (1997). Business Rules show Power, Promise. *Application Development Trends, 4* (3), 36-42.

Hay, D. & Healy, K.A. (1997). *GUIDE Business Rules Project, Final Report – revision 1.2.* Chicago: GUIDE International Corporation.

Hoffer, J.A., George, J.F., & Valacich, J.S. (1999). *Modern systems analysis and design* (2nd ed.). Reading, MA: Addison-Wesley Publishing Company.

Hurwitz, J. (1997). When rules meet development. *Database Programming & Design, 10* (1), 12-14.

Lawrence, B. (1998). Designers must do the modeling! *IEEE Software, 15* (2), 30-33.

Mahnic, V. (1997). Towards the re-integration of the University of Ljubljana information system. *Proceedings of European co-operation in higher education information systems.* Grenoble, France, September 1997, pp. 250-258

Mahnic, V., & Vilfan, B. (1995). Design of the student records information system at the University of Ljubljana. *Trends in academic information systems in Europe, Proceedings of the EUNIS'95 Congress.* Dusseldorf, Germany, 1995, pp. 207-220

McDonough, R. (1992). The management and administrative computing (MAC) initiative. *Higher Education Management, 4* (3), 284-292.

Powell, I.H.C. (1991). The MAC initiative in the United Kingdom. *CRE-action, 3*, 19-28.

Ross, R.G. (1997). *The business rule book: Classifying, defining and modelling rules.* Boston, MA: Database Research Group, Inc.

Rupnik, R., Bajec, M., & Krisper, M. (1997). Information system for application procedure for registration in higher education in Slovenia. *Proceedings of European co-operation in higher education information systems.* Grenoble, France, September 1997, pp.221-226.

Rymer, J.R. (1997). *Business rules: A promising technique, but not a new paradigm.* GIGA Information Group. [http://www.ilog.co.jp/html/products/infrastructure/rules_giga.htm]

Schutte, F. (1991). Information policy of Dutch university management. *CRE-action, 3*, 53-82.

Wild, P., & Fung, A. (1996). Evaluation of information technology in educational management for proactive development. *Education and Information Technologies*, 239-249.

5

Open ITEM Systems are Good ITEM Systems

A. Tatnall[1] and B. Davey[2]

[1] *School of Information Systems, Victoria University of Technology, Australia*

[2] *School of Information Technology, RMIT University, Australia*

Keywords: Educational Management, Infrastructure, Information Systems, Information Retrieval, Open Systems, Information Technology.

Abstract: Many educational authorities and third-party developers have, in the past, built ITEM (Information Technology and Educational Management) systems mainly for the benefit of central education authorities rather than schools. In some cases these systems have been designed without thorough consultation with schools. The result has been that many schools have not been able to get as much out of them as might otherwise have been possible.

Experience in designing the hardware and software components of business information systems has shown that *open systems*, in conjunction with formal software standards, are required to produce systems that can meet their full potential. It has also been shown that end-users will make much better use of systems that they have had a part in specifying. An inflexible system imposed from above is much less likely to be used effectively than one that clients are able to modify to suit their own requirements.

In this paper we advocate that future ITEM systems should be built as 'open systems' that can be adapted and modified by their users. In this we are arguing for much more than users just being able to select one of several pre-designed reports. What we are arguing for is systems that can be added to by the user, and that can be adapted to suit the users' own requirements.

1. INTRODUCTION

As the university travel department is running behind schedule, you have to pick up the airline tickets for your forthcoming conference trip yourself. You have driven into the city and parked next to a fire hydrant outside the travel agent's premises. When you come out after collecting your tickets you note a young woman smartly dressed in a City Council uniform standing next to your car, typing some data into a hand-held device with a short aerial. The device then prints out the parking ticket which she sticks onto your windscreen. It will do you no good trying to catch up with her to protest that you were in a hurry and were only parked there for a minute or two anyway, as your packing infringement has already been radioed through to the City Council's computer system.

A technician from Telstra[1] has just spent twenty minutes connecting your new computer network to a Telstra cable for fast Internet access. Before leaving, he types some numbers into a special device connected to his mobile phone. He then gets into his van and plugs this device and the mobile phone into its cradle before driving to his next assignment. When he starts the engine of the van the mobile phone automatically connects to Telstra's head office and up-loads details of the work he has just done at your site. The device also receives details of new jobs to be done later in the afternoon, and commences downloading another part of the new operating system to be installed in the van's computer next week.

The question we will address in this paper is why don't schools make use of technology like this for tasks like checking student attendance, operating library borrowing systems, running school sports meetings and entering student results? The answer is that to some extent, they do. It is possible to purchase systems using technology like PDA (Personal Digital Assistant) terminals and student swipe-cards for this purpose, but what tends to be missing from these systems is the link to the central database in the school administrative system. Our research has shown that although quite a number of Australian schools do use technology like this, they normally have to use it as a *separate system* unconnected with the school's main administrative system. These special systems operate separately largely due to the inflexibility of central ITEM systems, and the difficulty of using data from one system in the other, with the result that the same data is stored in multiple locations in each school.

2. SYSTEMS FOR RECORDING STUDENT ABSENCES

After encountering serious problems with student absences from class during the middle of the school day, Flower Meadows High School[2] implemented a new swipe-card system for recording student attendance. In this system students are issued with their own plastic ID card. Each card has the

[1] An Australian telephone company.

[2] A fictitious name for a real Australian school.

student's name, date of birth and photograph imprinted on the front, and a magnetic data stripe on the back. Each classroom has a card-reader at the door, and students swipe their ID card through this at the beginning of each class during the day. As the card-readers are networked back to the school administrative office, it is not difficult to see how the system could be used to record student attendance. Special software could then compare data from cards swiped though a card-reader each period with a central student database and print an exception report of student absences. The system could easily be programmed to flag special occurrences, such as when a student who is present in first period and absent in second and third periods is present again in period four. The system would then bring this information to the attention of relevant school staff.

Such a system is not new or particularly novel, and schools in several different countries successfully make use of technology like this (Selwood, 1996). In the case we are describing, however, there is a major difficulty, and when looked into further this becomes apparent. Flower Meadows needs to use the attendance system for initial entry of student enrolments as it must have new ID cards printed as early as possible. When enrolments have stabilised, the school then *prints* out class lists from the enrolment system and one of the office staff then *types* these into the main administrative system which is unable to accept external input other than via the keyboard.

Weir High School[3] issued all their teaching staff with a PDA (Palm Pilot III) at the start of the school year. Each PDA is loaded with special software and copies of student class lists for every class in the school, along with a copy of the school timetable. At the beginning of each period, teachers enter student absences (or lateness) into the device; it is presumed that all students not so marked are present. If a teacher is away then the replacement teacher who gets the 'extra' simply uses their own PDA which, like all the others, has been loaded with *all* the class lists. At the end of the day, or when a teacher has no more classes, they upload the absences into one of the PC data entry stations in each staffroom. As these PCs have been fitted with a special cradle to accommodate a PDA for data transfer, this is quite a simple task that normally takes only about 10 seconds.

During upload the system also checks to see when this PDA last had an update of its class lists, and whether there have been any changes since that time. If there have been changes a message appears on the PC screen asking the teacher to be patient and wait until new class lists have been downloaded to their device (Harper, 2000). After all teachers have uploaded their data, the central system is able to print out a series of reports, and lists of absences each period of the day.

[3] Another real Australian school with a fictitious name.

Although this is still a developing technology, some schools are also making use of this system on the portable PDAs on school excursions to ensure that no student gets left behind when the bus leaves. Others are entering disciplinary data such as when a student has been caught smoking, or fighting. Like the swipe-card system, however, the problem is that this system operates entirely separately from the school's central administrative system.

3. PROBLEMS WITH NON-INTEGRATED FUNCTIONAL SYSTEMS

Not only is the re-entry of data, required when using either of these systems, a waste of time and resources, but it also violates one of the main principles of database management (Date, 1983): that data should be stored in one place, and one place only. (It should be noted that there should always be a back-up copy of any database. What we are pointing out here is that there should only be one copy of the database *in use*.)

At this point a comparison with business information systems is useful. Traditionally, businesses have often been organised along *functional* lines. From early times, information systems were designed to support business functions such as accounting, manufacturing, finance, human resources, marketing and so on. In the early function-specific information systems, data was typically stored in file format, with data of a given type being stored in a particular file independently of all other data (Tatnall *et al.*, 2000). While these systems had their benefits, they also had problems (Reyes, 1998). For instance, data collected for use by one function-specific information system would typically not be available to another. This made systems of this type potentially quite inefficient. Specific information systems can, however, be designed to act together to produce an *integrated information system* whose purpose is to provide for the flow of information across all levels and functions of the organisation (Tatnall *et al.*, 2000). Data is stored once only, without duplication, and is able to support all activities relevant to the organisation, so improving communication between parts, or functions, of the organisation.

Using function-specific systems that are not integrated with the central database means that there will need to be multiple copies of the student database (for example), each of which must be frequently updated (Tatnall *et al.*, 2000). The difficulty is that when there are two or more different, unrelated student databases, any changes, such as new enrolments, changed student details and so on that occur, must be made to *each* database *every* time they occur. Human weakness means that with almost complete certainty, there will be a time when this does not occur and only one of the databases is updated. This means that the other database then becomes inaccurate.

The reason that Flower Meadows and Weir High Schools are unable to transfer the data from one system to the other is that the school administrative system that they both use has been designed as a function-specific system. It has been designed *not* to allow the importation of data from other systems, and not to allow other systems to directly access its own database. Presumably the designers of the school administrative system, provided by the Ministry of Education, had concerns about data security and integrity and so designed it that way. This system allows *download* of data, but nothing more.

4. WHO 'OWNS' THE ITEM SYSTEM?

In several Australian states, schools' administrative computing systems were built by central educational authorities and issued free (or at low cost) to schools. The primary motivation for doing this was to provide a reporting mechanism from schools back to the centre. Schools' administrative computing needs were not the main consideration (Tatnall, 1995). The general distribution of these systems to schools meant that schools could then be *instructed* that they *must* use them to provide the required reports back to the central authority.

While understanding why this approach was adopted, and not wanting to denigrate the needs of central educational authorities for information, we would argue that in future it would be much better if *individual schools*, rather than *school systems*, were seen as the prime clients by systems developers.

At issue here is who should be seen as the client. Who should the systems developers speak with about the systems requirements? There is a great deal of information systems literature that points to the necessity of involving users in the process of designing information systems (Fuller & William, 1994; Lindgaard, 1994; Alter, 1996; Lawrence *et al.*, 1997) if we want those systems to be used to their full potential. Lawrence *et al.* (1997) stress the need to consult with users, and Lindgaard (1994) notes that a large body of research has shown that potential users do not make best use of information systems unless they feel that these systems have been designed with their involvement and in their interest. Fuller and William (1994) point out that when business users think that central computing departments have been unresponsive to their needs they often take application development into their own hands, do their own thing, and ignore the central authority. If the central education authority is seen as the client then it is unlikely that schools will be entirely happy with the end product. It is more likely that they will do as Fuller and William suggest and bypass the central system.

There are many examples in business of information systems being designed for both central and local use. These systems can be built to offer the best of both worlds: a secure centralised database, combined with a degree of local autonomy in use. The technology and tools exist so that such systems need not compromise data security when offering local users some flexibility in how they use the data, and what other systems they allow to be connected. The theoretical advantages of such *integrated* systems (Tatnall & Davey, 1995) has been understood by those building business information systems for many years. The problem, rather, is one of system developers looking only to the central authority and not acknowledging that schools have differing information needs.

5. ISSUES OF DATA REDUNDANCY, CLOSED SYSTEMS AND INTEGRATION

At a first level of abstraction it is convenient to compare function-specific systems with integrated systems, but we will now look at what this means in practical terms. The main difference between having a number of unrelated functional systems and an integrated system is that in the first case, each system has its own database which is not shared with any other system, meaning that there is a great deal of data redundancy. The main issue then becomes: is the data stored in such a way that it can be accessed by the other systems? This does not necessarily imply *physically* storing all data in a single central database, but more likely would result in data stored in several locations that are *conceptually* linked together into a single database. If a system is set up this way it is comparatively easy to link in other functional systems at a later date.

To get an idea of the magnitude of the problem, imagine that a particular school has function-specific library borrowing, student attendance, student results and sports meeting systems as well as its central administrative system. As each of these systems involves lists of students there will need to be *five* separate, unrelated copies of the student database maintained and used in the school. When a student transfers into or out of the school, five different databases need to be updated. This can be done by just updating the central system then downloading this data again to each of the other systems but, however it is done, it is a substantial and time wasting task that has lots of potential for going wrong, with the result that one or more of the databases becomes corrupted or not updated properly. Carefully choice of additional functional systems that are able to co-operate and share data can reduce this difficulty (Athey *et al.*, 1991; Selwood, 1996), but the problem of an inflexible central system still remains.

When the initial system is built as a closed system that allows no other systems access to its data, except perhaps by download, data integration and the use of a single common database is not possible. In the cases we have highlighted, both the system using PDAs and that using the swipe-cards are function-specific. Both were purchased from third-party commercial suppliers who were unable to integrate their systems with the ITEM system provided by the central education authority as this was designed as a closed system. The result is data duplication and waste.

6. PREDICTING EACH SCHOOL'S FUTURE INFORMATION NEEDS

Many of the ITEM systems used in managing schools around the world are good, well designed systems. Unfortunately, however, some were designed primarily to satisfy the information needs of central education authorities (Tatnall, 1995) and others appear to have been designed on the premise that the designers knew all about schools' information needs and so need not offer any third-party expansion options. What is more, the use of such a closed, proprietary-like approach means that they are also premised on the assumption that the designers alone will be able to modify them to satisfy future needs. It assumes that the designers know what schools will need in the future, and that they will be able to incorporate these changes into their systems. On this premise they construct closed systems that schools cannot add to or change. This creates a problem that Frank and Fulmer (1998:94) put this way: "...it is a common experience that the information systems developer who limits development to working with what is instead of what should be has created a static system that is outdated and serves only to audit a system going nowhere."

Because schools are different, their information needs are also different. Flower Meadows and Weir High Schools each saw the need to develop attendance systems, and each came up with a different solution. As the designers of the central ITEM system did not foresee any need for schools to use solutions for student attendance other than the one they had provided, they did not offer the facility for other systems to connect to theirs. They did allow data *download*, but nothing more. In similar vein there are many other situations in which a systems designer could not possibly come up with a perfect solution that would be suitable for all schools into the future. Perhaps the ITEM system provided to a school does not link in with the library borrowing system, perhaps it does not handle school sports and the school wants to add this feature, perhaps it handles lateness in a way that is not appropriate for this particular school, perhaps it needs to do something else that no one has thought of yet. In these events, we would argue that the ITEM software should empower (Davey & Reyes, 1998) an individual school by enabling it to make appropriate changes in the way the software operates, or to add new systems to work with, and be integrated with, the one provided.

We acknowledge that not all schools will be able, or even want, to modify these systems, but argue that this facility should be available to them. This is often not the case at present.

7. ALTERNATIVE APPROACHES AND RECOMMENDATIONS

We have argued that ITEM systems must be open systems that allow the easy integration of new third party products where appropriate. Within this constraint, many different open architectures are possible, but some form of client-server or distributed database (Davey & Tatnall, 1997; Davey & Reyes, 1998) offering read-only access to some tables of the central database would probably be best (Tatnall & Tatnall, 1998). The important point is that only one copy of data, such as lists of students and teaching staff, should be kept. The system should be open to *accredited*, conforming applications to have read/write access to this data, while other (non-conforming) applications should be granted read-only access. Such a system could look something like the diagram in Figure 1 below.

As well as the central database, use could be made of a data warehouse that could be set up to allow any users (accredited or not) easy and rapid access to specialised queries on selected data.

For any access like this to be possible, however, the data should be stored in a commonly accessible format. An ODBC format useable by database systems like Microsoft Access, and programming languages like Visual Basic is preferable as it means that users and third-party developers can easily access this data via other custom-designed programs. The data structure must be clearly set out and documented, with information and help for potential school developers. Documentation on the operation and design of the system should be clear, and should be written at a number of different levels suitable for users, school-level developers, and third-party developers.

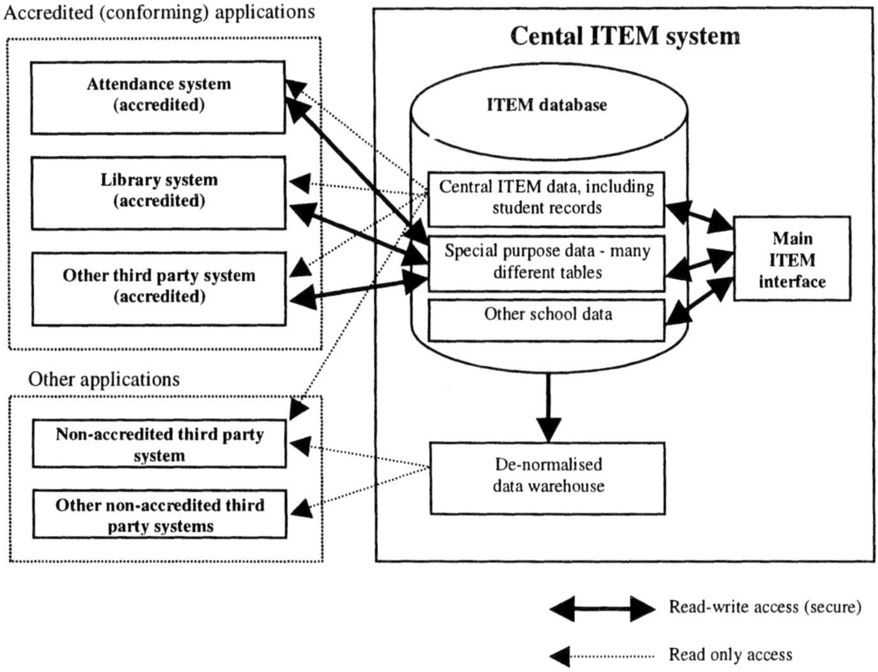

Figure 1: An architecture for an open ITEM system

8. CONCLUSION

Generally speaking, the current generation of ITEM systems are well designed functional systems that provide useful reports, and the standard operations that the designers thought that schools might require. New systems will, however, need to do more. Future systems will need to offer facilities and perform tasks that neither schools nor developers have thought of yet. To do this these new systems must be open and flexible so that they can be easily extended. They must also be able to interface easily with other third-party systems not yet designed. Systems designers can't predict the future, but they can allow for it by making their systems open.

We argue that if future ITEM systems are open systems that incorporate features of this sort they will be a lot more useful to their ultimate clients – schools.

REFERENCES

Alter, S. (1996). *Information systems: A management perspective* (2nd ed.). Menlo Park, CA: Benjamin Cummins.

Athey, T.H., Day, J.C., & Zmud, R.W. (1991). *Computers and end-user software*. New York: Harper Collins.

Date, C.J. (1983). *Database: A primer*. USA: Addison Wesley.

Davey, B., & Tatnall, A. (1997). Distributed ITEM for the future: Moving towards client-server systems. In A.C.W. Fung, A.J. Visscher, B.Z. Barta, & D.C.B. Teather (Eds.), *Information technology in educational management for the schools of the future*. London: Chapman & Hall.

Davey, B., & Reyes, G. (1998). Overcoming resistance to integration: using client-server systems and data warehousing. In C.L. Fulmer, B.Z. Barta, & P. Nolan (Eds.), *The integration of information for educational management*. Whitefield, Maine: Felicity Press.

Frank, F.P., & Fulmer, C.L. (1998). The dysfunctional side of educational organizations: Themes from clinical information systems development. In C.L. Fulmer, B.Z. Barta, & P. Nolan (Eds.), *The integration of information for educational management*. Whitefield, Maine: Felicity Press.

Fuller, F., & William, M. (1994). *Computers and information processing*. Massachusetts: Boyd & Fraser.

Harper, R. (2000). *A breakthrough in attendance monitoring and reporting*. Australia: RollCall. [http://www.rollcall.Australia.au]

Lawrence, D.R., Shah, H.U., & Golder, P.A. (1997). Business users and the information systems development process. In B.Z. Barta, A. Tatnall, & P. Juliff (Eds.), *The place of information technology in management and business education*. London: Chapman & Hall.

Lindgaard, G. (1994). Usability testing and system evaluation. London: Chapman & Hall.

Reyes, M.G. (1998). A model illustrating the implication of information integration on educational administration. In C.L. Fulmer, B.Z. Barta, & P. Nolan (Eds.), *The integration of information for educational management*. Whitefield, Maine: Felicity Press.

Selwood, I.D. (1996). Information technology to record and monitor school attendance. In A.C.W. Fung, A.J. Visscher, B.Z. Barta, & D.C.B. Teather (Eds.), *Information technology in educational management for the schools of the future*. London: Chapman & Hall.

Tatnall, A. (1995). Information technology and the management of Victorian schools: Providing flexibility or enabling better central control? In B.Z. Barta, M. Telem, & Y. Gev (Eds.), *Information technology in educational management*. London, Chapman & Hall.

Tatnall, A., & Davey, B. (1995). Executive information systems in school management: A research perspective. In J.D. Tinsley, & T.J. van Weert (Eds.), *World Conference on Computers in Education VI. WCCE'95. Liberating the learner*. London: Chapman & Hall.

Tatnall, A., Davey, B., Burgess, S., *et al.* (2000). *Management information systems: Concepts, issues, tools and applications* (2nd ed.). Melbourne: Data Publishing.

Tatnall, A., & Tatnall, B. (1998). Data integration in a training institute: Modelling a client-server solution. In C.L. Fulmer, B.Z. Barta, & P. Nolan (Eds.), *The integration of information for educational management*. Whitefield, Maine: Felicity Press.

6

Information Systems for Leading and Managing Schools: Changing the Paradigm

C.J. P. Nolan and M. Lambert
Massey University, Palmerston North, New Zealand
Fax: +64 6 3513325
E-mail: P.Nolan@massey.ac.nz

Key words: Information Systems, Schools as Organisations, Learning Community, Paradigm Shift, School Case Studies

Abstract: Although schools in New Zealand have long viewed themselves, and functioned, as organisations, experience and research show that they must, in the future, increasingly develop and operate as learning communities to be educationally effective. This paper examines the extent to which three schools have been able to employ a widely used state of the art computerised information system in ways that support their operation and development as learning communities. Findings, from case studies of the schools, show that two factors are key in enabling school personnel to use the system effectively: (1) the strength of commitment by school leaders and teachers to learning community principles, and (2) the technical understanding and know-how of the principal particularly and, to a lesser extent, the staff, rather than system characteristics or design features. Discussion suggests new directions for the design of computerised school information systems and the need to reformulate common understandings of what might count as "good systems" for schools that either operate, or aspire to operate, as learning communities.

1. INTRODUCTION

Over the last ten years in New Zealand, the adoption and use of computerised school information systems (CSIS) has dramatically increased. The manner in which they are used, however, varies markedly between schools (Nolan and Ayres, 1996). Moreover, a correlation seems to exist between types of school culture and use patterns. For instance, secondary schools tend to have more teachers than primary schools with the capability and experience to use a wide range of administrative and management programs. It seems, though, that they use them to perform quite specific one-off tasks, reflecting perhaps the segmented organisational cultures of secondary schools. Moreover, when the programs are used to carry out higher order functions, this activity tends to be confined within a school's management team. In contrast, it is far more common for primary schools, using somewhat fewer computer resources, to make key data about the school (*e.g.* details of the school budget) available to the whole staff, reflecting thereby a sense of community more than organisation. In a primary school, as community, the collaborative solving of problems and the shared making of decisions tend to prevail. In secondary schools, this approach is not well understood and it appears, as yet, to be seldom used (Nolan and Ayres, 1996).

Beyond these global variations, all schools in New Zealand share the common attribute of having to meet mandated requirements emanating from government policies of school accountability. Over the last decade or more, schools have been required by law to regularly submit reports on many aspects of school operations, assess student achievement and report results against pre-specified achievement objectives, and demonstrate that mandated programme delivery requirements have been met. The methods of accountability are enshrined in the Government's National Education and Administration Guidelines (NEGS and NAGS) that detail specifically the requirements to be met and the manner of meeting them. Designers of computerised systems have responded accordingly by providing schools with the kinds of administrative and management programs they require. These are capable of both the automating and informating functions identified by Visscher (1996), but it is conjectured here that their utility lies more in how they assist schools to demonstrate accountability than support school development.

The dramatic increase of CSIS adoption and use mentioned above has undoubtedly caused schools to change their administrative and management systems in line with the NEGS and NAGS, with consequent internal changes to organisational functioning as well. The extent and nature of the latter varies by type of school and by school level (Ayres, Nolan and Visscher, 1998). It could be said that the organisational functioning of schools nationally has stabilised around varyingly low to high levels of computerised administrative efficiency and effectiveness in meeting the requirements that have been persistently made of them. Moreover, schools have developed adroitness in the computerised management of information (Visscher, 1996), although the adroitness undoubtedly varies between schools.

As in most countries, New Zealand schools are always subject to political whim. The lessons of recent history say that schools must be on guard constantly to ensure that systems and procedures, along with the culture and organisation of the school, are sufficiently robust to manage change that can be mandated by government at any point. This is especially the case at times when the government changes, as it did it late 1999.

If government guidelines of the last decade defined an "accountability for outcomes" and a "compliance" role for school administration and management, changes to them in early 2000, immediately following the change of government, now specify that schools will exercise "accountability for processes" rather than outcomes, as their first priority. One might argue that the focus now will be much more on developing the technical core of the school (Fulmer, 1995), i.e. the enhancement of learning and teaching, improvement to the quality of programmes, and the utilisation of computerised school information systems to these ends.

In this enterprise, the definition of school management is likely also to change, with greater value being placed on the exercise of educational leadership whose purpose is to achieve educational ends as much as accountability ones. At the school level, the shift is, in effect, a shift from educational organisation to learning community as the paramount concept behind the work of a school.

By implication, a shift will be required in the design of computerised school information systems away from the organisational and accountability system concepts of the past and towards classroom-focused information systems (Frank and Fulmer, 1998). In New Zealand, this shift is already happening, but in making it system designers appear to have retained the underlying spreadsheet and data base design approaches and philosophy that they have used habitually in the past. The software produced for teachers by application of these approaches and philosophy has enormous "processing power". Senior school managers and administrators and some teachers are increasingly applying this power to enhance the professionalism of teachers working in the "technical core". But anecdotal reports indicate that teachers are struggling to adapt and use to good effect software programs and systems that were, in effect, designed for a different purpose, i.e. to meet accountability demands.

2. PURPOSE

In this paper we present case studies of three schools which function, by and large, as learning communities. The studies report how the schools are attempting to implement, though not without difficulty, "state of the art" computerised school information system programs, of the kind referred to above, to support their learning community focus and develop it further.

Discussion of findings from the studies: (1) examines directions for computerised school information system design of the future; (2) proposes modifications to our understanding of what might count as a "good system"; and (3) suggests ways that leadership and management, supported by use of computerised systems, might better assist the development of schools as learning communities in the future.

3. METHOD

The particular schools were selected for two main reasons. Firstly, they operate in ways that experience, policy and research suggest schools might operate and develop in the future as learning communities (see the discussion below that illustrates the learning community concept). Secondly, they were judged to be typical of schools that both perceive themselves, and are perceived by others, as effective users of computerised school information systems. The case studies illustrate the efforts by the schools to implement effective development and implementation practices. They do not, and could not, document the full range of good development and implementation practice and they do not deal with "unsuccessful" practices, other than in the sense of documenting difficulties encountered and problematic aspects of use. In this respect, the studies simply begin the process of systematically researching the development and implementation challenges that schools and system developers will face and have to address in the future.

Data were collected through direct observations and first hand accounts of system adoption, implementation and use in each school. These were augmented by focused, in-depth interviews with the full range of individuals involved, including school board members, teachers and school administrators, directly and indirectly associated with developments, support agency staff and system developers. The case studies summarise the data in the form of accounts of the situation in each school regarding the role and effects of the computerised information systems.

4. BACKGROUND

Primary schools were studied because they best illustrate the concept of learning community in action whereas secondary schools operate more typically as organisations and only in rare instances as communities. In the New Zealand education system, primary schools cater, in the main, for the needs of children aged between 5 and 11 years and they range in size from 1-

2 teachers to 30+ teachers. The schools of this study are of comparable size (approximately 10 teachers and 200 students each) and they all use the MUSAC (Massey University School Administration by Computer) school information system, but vary slightly with respect to the specific programs used.

MUSAC software is used in over 2000 schools, or 75% of all New Zealand schools. The MUSAC system, a comprehensive and integrated suite of programs (see the MUSAC website – http://musac.massey.ac.nz – for a full description), has been re-designed over the past three years to include programs for teacher as well as administrator use. It encompasses all aspects of the administration and management of schools as outlined in the School Information System Framework developed by Visscher (1996) and it includes specific programs teachers can use in their classrooms and other work places to support curriculum planning and delivery. In this respect, the MUSAC system conforms to the concept of a classroom focused information system (Frank & Fulmer, 1998). Moreover, previous research (Nolan & Ayres, 1996) has demonstrated that the MUSAC system satisfies the technical criteria of a "good system" in that it can be employed to "collect data, automate processes and informate the work of multiple decision makers from different organisational levels" (Fulmer, 1995). Its bottom-up design and incorporation of a help desk and a user group facility means that the system is responsive to user needs.

All three schools commonly employ the generic MUSAC *Pupil Files* database program which stores the full gamut of student demographic and personal data (*e.g.* name, address, caregivers, age, siblings, health). Data in *Pupil Files* may be integrated with data from all other programs. It permits the seamless transfer of information between programs and comparative and correlational analyses of data from different programs, *e.g.* absences related to test scores and participation in sport correlated with academic performance. The case studies document the ways in which each school complements its use of *Pupil Files* with other programs. These include:

- *Progress Monitor* for recording and analysing data on all aspects of student performance;
- *Library Manager* for managing all aspects of the operation of the school library including student use and borrowing patterns; and
- *Classroom Manager* for supporting teacher management of classroom curriculum programmes and school-wide programme planning and review.

5. LEARNING COMMUNITIES IN ACTION

All three schools exhibit in their mode of operation, and in their cultures, features that identify them as learning communities. These features include:

1. Activities that establish and develop, as necessary, shared understandings, beliefs and values central to the school culture;
2. The collective determination of school wide goals, priorities and directions;
3. The delegation of responsibility to teacher syndicates for all curriculum planning, implementation and review;
4. Collaborative development of the school budget and the allocation of resources by consensus; and
5. Collegial review of programmes within and across syndicate boundaries and staff workshops to identify and share best practices regarding learning, teaching and the assessment of student performance.

While these features predominate to a greater or lesser extent in all three schools, each school also functions to some extent as an organisation in respect to:

1. Meeting mandated requirements (*e.g.* submitting monthly financial reports to the School Board and quarterly reports of students enrolled to the Ministry of Education); and
2. Ensuring, day to day, that routine administrative tasks are executed efficiently, *e.g.* the production of myriad lists relating to, for example, class scheduling and the organisation of extra curricula activities, the operation of the school library and tracking the flow of shared teaching resources between classrooms and syndicates.

By and large, senior administrators and office staff use the MUSAC software programs identified above to perform the administrative work of making their schools function smoothly as "organisations". The extent and frequency of their use in this way varies between the schools. The variation, in its turn, reflects differences between school personnel in familiarity with the software and corresponding differences in their competency and confidence to use it. Teaching staff in each school are encouraged to employ the software, or outputs generated by it, in relation to features which identify the schools as learning communities, though with varying success as detailed below in the case study accounts.

In each school, the principal plays a key role encouraging staff at all levels to develop the knowledge and skills they need. The exercise of this role by the principal distinguishes the three schools from many, perhaps most, other primary schools. This is because, in the schools selected for study, the principals have a clearly developed vision of the role that a CSIS might play and they clearly articulate the vision to staff and the school community. Decisions regarding software and hardware acquisition are taken either by the staff as a whole or by the principal in consultation with the staff.

This approach is consistent with the notion of community, in which no one person has the right to make unilateral decisions on matters that affect the welfare and development of the community and its members. In this respect, all the schools operate a form of "citizen democracy" (Saul, 1995). That is to say, all members are accorded respect as persons and as capable professionals and the power and authority associated with particular positions is downplayed in favour of a more collegial approach.

A variety of factors appear to affect the way in which CSIS use can, and actually does, facilitate the realisation of "citizen democracy" in each school and assist them to function effectively as communities in the full sense to which they each aspire. The factors include: features of the software, *e.g.* its design philosophy and approach and user support strategies; the levels and kinds of CSIS knowledge and capability distributed among staff; attitudes of support or resistance among staff; and the organisational and cultural conditions prevalent in each school.

The case studies provide accounts of the way that the factors, both on their own and in interaction with each other, are pressing the schools to operate and develop in particular directions. The overall modus operandi of each school is indicated by its location on the diagonal in Figure 1 below. The diagonal is the dividing line that distinguishes a school that operates predominantly as an organisation from one that operates as a learning community. This way of depicting the difference captures the idea that while any given school may operate predominantly as a community, it will contain, inevitably, organisational elements, *e.g.* as reflected in the presence of hierarchical management positions, even though the importance of these may be de-emphasised.

Use of the diagonal in this way indicates the present modus operandi, but suggests the possibility that while a school may be operating in a particular way at any given time, its mode of operation may change and thus its location on the diagonal. This may happen for any one or a number of reasons, *e.g.* the appointment of staff members who subscribe to a different view or the implementation of a school development process. As Figure 1 shows, location of the three schools at the top of the diagonal indicates that they presently operate as learning communities in the manner described above.

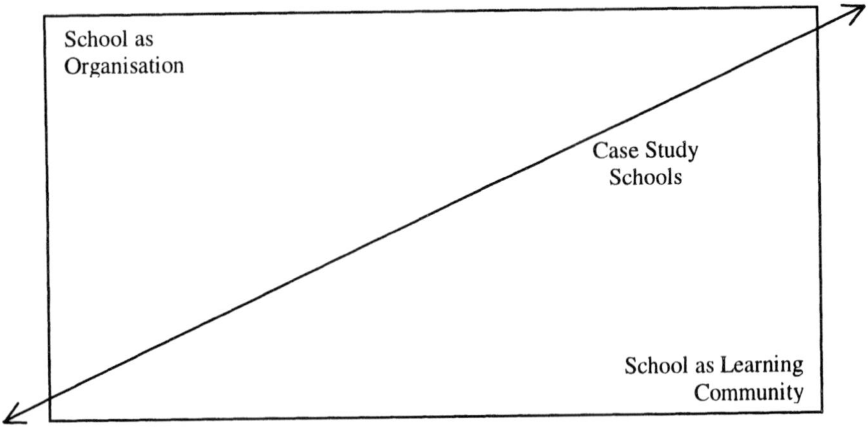

Figure 1. Model of school operation and development

6. CASE STUDIES

6.1 School One

During school-wide review and planning meetings at year's end and at the beginning of each new school year, the staff of School One collaboratively develops year-long learning and teaching programmes to be implemented across the whole school. The programmes reflect a staff consensus that designated learning areas and skills should feature centrally in any given year. For instance, the staff as a whole decided that the development of self-esteem, literacy and numeracy should feature centrally as school wide themes in 2000. In this way the staff as whole addressed specific needs that were identified by the school community at the end of the preceding year as requiring special and ongoing attention. To this end, the school both adopted and adapted two MUSAC programs, *Progress Monitor* and *Pupil Files*, to generate the data and information on student performance that both the school and parents would need.

The programs were adopted because, in tandem, they provide the means to store, correlate and analyse student performance data generated from three main sources linked to:

1. Teacher-defined achievement objectives for the various essential learning areas and essential skills of the national curriculum, along with literacy, numeracy and self-esteem objectives;

2. Learning goals and associated objectives developed by the students and incorporated into classroom programmes; and
3. Standardised tests in a range of key areas, *e.g.* National Progressive Achievement Tests in Reading, Mathematics and Study Skills and School Entry Assessment.

Data from the standardised tests provide the school administrators, as well as teachers, with an independent measure of student progress. Interestingly, in this school, the principal himself enters the performance data from each source into the MUSAC *Classroom Manager* program. Additionally, the principal utilised *Classroom Manager* to institute and maintain a school-wide register of extra and co-curricula activities and interests, along with special needs information to reflect the school's learning community philosophy to develop the whole child.

The programs had to be adapted, however, because the principal and staff considered that default output, in the form of numerical tables and graphs, was an inappropriate way, on its own, to record and report student progress and performance. This was especially so in light of school policy to use student portfolios for assessment, and compile "annual assessment profiles" for each student. The latter served also as a cumulative achievement record to be transported from one class level to the next and between schools. It proved to be particularly useful with children who returned to the school after a period elsewhere.

The production of these profiles necessitated the special "tailoring" of *Progress Monitor* output so as to produce meaningful information for teacher use and reports that were comprehensible to parents. For instance, in order to illustrate specific accomplishments and progress, along with learning difficulties, in the various learning areas, anecdotes were incorporated in reports through the use of additional (adjunct) functions especially inserted into the program by the developer. These especially created functions are *Progress Monitor* "templates" used to construct annual assessment profiles. If the CSIS is well utilised, this is due in large measure to the determination of the principal and staff to make the system fit the school rather than the school fit the system.

This school routinely implements a school-wide school development process to review programmes, share best practices, and develop shared understandings around values, goals and directions. The process relies heavily on such techniques as narrative accounts, story telling and the summation of written reports, including ideas and resources gleaned from the professional literature on school and curriculum development and allied topics. Yet, little if any of this work is supported by the CSIS. The explanation given by the principal and various staff is that the system does not lend itself readily to processing qualitative data and information germane to their school development and improvement processes.

6.2 School Two

In School Two, the principal developed and promoted school-wide, and in the school community, a view that education with ICT (information and communication technology) should feature increasingly in school programmes. ICT should be used primarily as tools for learning, but also as administration and management tools that teachers could employ for school decision making and the development of school policy. Over time, this view was incorporated into school policy and in the three years since the principal's appointment, all computers available for teacher use (one per teacher) were upgraded and networked. Consistent with school policy, both teachers and administrative staff are being provided with the professional development and training they need, although this is less with CSIS than with learning and teaching applications.

MUSAC *Pupil Files*, used extensively for the past six years, and MUSAC *Progress Monitor*, used for the last three, are now employed in tandem in a manner similar to School One. MUSAC *Library Manager* is utilised mainly as a stand alone library administration and management tool, with its integration capabilities being employed from time to time for school wide purposes, *e.g.* analysis of class borrowing patterns linked to family circumstances such as socio-economic status and ethnicity. Such a use is evidence of the principal's growing ability to utilise the informating functions of the software. Unlike the principal of School One, however, his approach is to generate standard numerical and graphing reports to show trends and patterns.

Both the principal and staff are aware that such use, unless carefully controlled, can produce data and information for its own sake rather than serve a useful purpose such as to inform decisions or help develop policy. For example, in 1999, the whole staff reported and recorded swimming ability levels "which they graphed in many ways". They came to see this as futile, however, because their analyses produced results that served no useful purpose!

Although this school operates by and large as a learning community, the use of the CSIS reflects more nearly an organisational model, as shown perhaps in its predominant use by the principal for addressing accountability requirements, and corresponding use by staff to complete standardised forms. This is not to gainsay the fact that the school and its staff operate effectively as a community, and, in contrast with CSIS use, ICT is generally integrated well into classroom practice.

6.3 School Three

In this school, the principal has a developing vision of the role that a CSIS might play to support administration and management functions and the role of ICT as providing educational tools. The vision is based upon many years of experience of using computers and helping others to use them. Recently, the school was commended by the Educational Review Office as a "moving school" in the sense of demonstrating collaborative professional development practices linked to ICT. These are promoted and encouraged by the principal and they are the means by which staff members assist each other to develop awareness and mastery of the administrative and management tools available to them in the MUSAC *Classroom Manager* program. The collaborative practices include: peer coaching, externally facilitated training workshops, team meetings to share good ideas, planning cooperatively how to use the program, and an informal "buddy system" to support self directed learning.

The professional development programme is a key means by which the staff, working with the principal, is developing a shared vision for the implementation and use of information technology school-wide, including a plan for use of the CSIS. Two specific developments are occurring simultaneously: (1) installation of an intra-net for linking all computers school-wide and then providing all teachers with remote access to the CSIS; and (2) ongoing professional development and training to increase the skills of both teachers and administrative staff in CSIS implementation and use (see Nolan, Ayres and McKinnon, 1996 for an account of the staff development strategies employed).

The vision, developed internally, is being adopted by the School Board of Trustees and they, along with the principal and staff, are promoting the vision in the school community as signaling a preferred direction for future school development.

In this development, the principal and the staff, working together, are gradually translating the overall vision into commitment to:

1. Generate documentation for parents that report student progress quarterly;
2. Gather data and information, especially on student achievement and attitudes, more objective than that presently available;
3. Identify and record systematically the learning needs of students through consultation with caregivers and the students themselves, and link the needs thus identified with national achievement objectives as specified in National Curriculum Statements; and

4. Develop computerised procedures to record, monitor and report student progress against school-based achievement criteria, as well as (and in time perhaps as an alternative to) the normative criteria of national standardised tests.

By moving the school in these directions, the principal and staff indicate their more deep-seated commitment to learning community goals and objectives. This is reflected specifically in the principal's goal to replace, in a relatively short time, conventional computer generated reports with digital portfolios. This development is currently being frustrated through lack of CSIS capability to produce the desired result.

7. CONCLUSIONS

At the 1998 ITEM Working Conference, one participant warned that continuing to design CSISs for existing educational structures, simply making the structures more efficient than they are now, is likely to inhibit change and development, not promote it (Nolan *et al.*, 1998). The case studies illustrate how three schools, wanting to change and develop, found that their state of the art systems helped them to administer and manage efficiently but often did not provide the means to review and develop programmes or chart new directions at the school level. Principals and other school personnel commonly saw use value in conventional spreadsheet generated results and information, *e.g.* reports on the academic progress of students. They also commonly required other kinds of results and information, however, that their existing systems could not readily produce, *e.g.* the digitised portfolios referred to in Case Study 3.

Findings from the case studies reported here support conclusions of the 1998 Conference delegates that "good" CSISs of the future must:

1. Incorporate in their designs a social vision of school which empowers rather constrains learners and teachers (sic, dramatically more than is possible now with existing systems);
2. Embody design concepts broad enough to accommodate the full range of information contained in schools; and
3. Build in features which increase the likelihood that stakeholders' rights of access to, and use of, information can be realised.

The incorporation of these features in system designs of the future would be consistent with the findings of contemporary school development research (Day, 2000; Hopkins *et al.*, 1994; Sergiovanni, 1996; Stewart *et al.*, 1997) and the experience of the schools reported in this paper. That is to say, schools must increasingly operate as learning communities with shared decision making and shared access to the data and information upon which the making of decisions is based. Such a shift will require an adjustment in our basic assumptions and thinking about the nature and operation of educational institutions, and their computerised information systems, that is akin to a paradigm shift (Kuhn, 1970).

Findings from all three case studies show that two factors are key in enabling school personnel to use their existing systems effectively and take initial steps towards making the paradigm shift: (1) the strength of commitment by school leaders and teachers to learning community principles, and (2) the technical understanding and know-how of the principal particularly and, to a lesser extent, the staff rather than system characteristics or design features (Visscher, 1996).

For instance, in School One, the principal used his technical knowledge to adapt the CSIS, thereby enabling him and other staff members to operate the school along learning community lines, for example by incorporating student nominated achievement objectives into curriculum programmes and assessment procedures. In School Two, the system was *adopted* and implemented "as is" by the principal and staff. They were no less committed to the learning community model, but their lack of technical knowledge constrained them from using the system in support of learning community goals to the same extent. An unintended effect was that the principal's management and leadership style became more "organisationally orientated" than he realised or intended. In School Three, the principal, who understood the shortcomings of the system, knowingly adopted it but he did so with the explicit realisation that it would have to be modified.

An important implication of the studies is that senior school personnel and teachers must be acknowledged to be now, and in the future, the key factor in the ability of schools to effectively and fully utilise their (expensive) computerised systems to support the operation and development of schools. This is the case for two reasons.

Firstly, these personnel either possess or can learn the technical skills required. This aspect of the situation must not be under-rated. Even though designers strive to make their systems user friendly and intuitively useable, their effective use will require technical competency and confidence much more than can be acquired just by reading a manual or picking up the necessary knowledge by word of mouth. A further implication, then, is that schools must be prepared to invest in the professional development of staff much more than in the past.

Secondly, school personnel (teachers, senior administrators and managers, and office staff especially) understand the nature of the data and information they need upon which to make informed judgements and decisions about directions for development at classroom, programme and school levels. These data and information encompass much more than is typically permitted by school administration and management software designed around conventional alpha/numeric database and spreadsheet formats. Such formats, now intrinsic to good software designs, will remain so. But, the designs of the future will be much broader in scope and more accommodating than they are now of the inherent complexity, sophistication and subtlety of professional life and work in educational institutions.

By and large, the effect of New Zealand's National Education and Administration Guidelines, imposed by successive governments, has been to focus the attention of school leaders and managers on meeting accountability expectations, operating the school smoothly as an organisation and producing results. Teachers have been expected to assess students against a myriad of pre-set Achievement Objectives. The conscientious execution of this task has directed their attention, and that of school leaders also, towards performance as an organisation and away from ways by which to function better as learning communities. In the climate that has produced this effect, teachers are trusted less as responsible professionals, they are expected to comply with externally imposed expectations, and professional commitment is valued less than in the past. Compliance has tended to replace consent as a motive for action. The computerised school information systems designed and developed in this climate have, by and large, embodied principles and precepts consistent with the concept of the school as an organisation – generating mandated returns, processing normative data, and calculating and reporting performance statistics.

Computerised systems for schools of the future may still be required for these purposes. Increasingly their purpose will be to support, however, development in ways that take account of and deal with the complexity, sophistication and subtlety mentioned above. As this development unfolds, educational professionals at all levels will review and reflect upon their practice and strive to improve it. In this enterprise, narrative and stories will increasingly become the objects of analysis and communication using computerised systems somewhat more sophisticated and multi-media capable than they are now.

REFERENCES

Ayres, D., Nolan, C.J.P., & Visscher, A.J. (1998). Computer-based school information systems: Researching New Zealand use patterns and levels of use. In C.L. Fulmer, C.J.P. Nolan, & B.Z. Barta (Eds.), *The integration of information for educational management.* Whitefield, Maine: Felicity Press.

Day, C. (2000). Beyond transformational leadership. *Educational Leadership, 57* (7), 56-59.

Frank, F.P., & Fulmer, C.L. (1998). Paper presented at the *International Working Conference on Information Technology and Educational Management.* Christmas Cove, Maine, USA.

Fulmer, C.L. (1995). Maximising the potential of information technology for management strategies for interfacing the technical core of education. In B.Z. Barta, M. Telem, & Y. Gev (Eds.) *Information technology in educational management.* London: Chapman Hall.

Hopkins, D., Ainscow, M., & West, M. (1994). *School improvement in an era of change.* London: Cassell.

Kuhn, T.S. (1970). *The structure of scientific revolutions.* Chicago: Chicago University Press.

Nolan, C.J.P., & Ayres, D.A. (1996). Developing a "good" information for schools: The New Zealand experience. *International Journal of Educational Research, 25* (5), 307-319.

Nolan, C.J.P., Fulmer C.L., & Taylor, R.G. (1998). Four computerised school information systems: Summary discussion. In C.L. Fulmer, C.J.P. Nolan, & B.Z. Barta (Eds.), *The integration of information for educational management.* Whitefield, Maine: Felicity Press.

Saul. J.R. (1995). *The unconscious civilization.* Concord, Ontario: House of Anansi Press.

Sergiovanni, T.J. (1996). *Leadership for the schoolhouse: How is it different? Why is it important?* San Francisco: Jossey-Bass Publishers.

Stewart, D.J., Prebble, T., & Duncan, P. (1997). *The reflective principal: Leading the school development process.* Katonah, New York: Richard C. Owen Publishers.

Visscher, A.J. (1996). Information technology in educational management as an emerging discipline. *International Journal of Educational Research, 25* (4), 291-296.

7

CSIS Usage in School Management: A Comparison of Good and Bad Practice Schools

A.J. Visscher and P.P.M. Bloemen
University of Twente, Faculty of Educational Science and Technology, Department of Educational Organisation and Management

Key words: School Information System, System Utilisation, School Management

Abstract: Although the implementation and use of computerised information systems is quite common in developed countries, they are mainly limited to clerical types of support. The utilisation of the potential of these systems by school management is far below what seems possible. In this study, a group of twelve schools, including good and bad practice schools, has been investigated to obtain a more detailed picture of how school managers work with these information systems and which factors seem to promote managerial system usage. System use proves to vary considerably between schools, and five factors seem to have a promoting influence in the good practice schools. Recommendations have been formulated on the basis of the results to promote the managerial use of school information systems.

1. INTRODUCTION AND PROBLEM STATEMENT

Research has shown that nearly all Dutch schools for secondary education have a computer-assisted school information system supporting clerical work in schools. The support of managerial activities proves to be very limited (Visscher, 1992 & 1997; Visscher & Bloemen, 1999). This is not unique for the Netherlands, but is a problem worldwide (Ayres *et al.*, 1998; Visscher *et al.*, 1999) and regrettable since schools in many countries receive more discretion to develop their own school policies. The growing autonomy of schools implies that they need to develop plans in areas where they formerly could execute policies developed at national levels. This requires that school staff acquire new skills, and get information on which they can base their policies. Computerised information systems can assist here by providing valuable management information. The thousand dollar question remains how the full utilisation of these systems can be accomplished.

Research into the factors promoting the use of clerical systems is limited, whereas the picture regarding the factors determining managerial system usage is even worse. Actually, we do not know of any empirical study into this topic. Therefore, this research project explores how school managers in good practice and in bad practice schools (as far as computer-assisted school management is concerned) use their computer system, and which factors seem to explain their being outliers on the positive or negative side. More specifically, the following research questions guided this study:

1. To what extent and how do school managers in good practice and bad practice schools use computer-assisted school information systems for managerial work?
2. Which factors seem to promote the managerial usage of computer-assisted school information systems?

The answers to these questions were expected to form a basis for formulating guidelines, to help schools gain higher levels of computer-assisted school management.

2. THEORETICAL FRAMEWORK

This study did not focus on structured managerial problems (for example, the construction of the timetable) for which a limited number of variables and solutions are typical, since the use of computers for solving these problems does not seem to be difficult. The research concentrated on the use of school information systems for ill-structured school management problems characterised by uncertain causes, a large number of variables that (often in combination with each other) may cause a problem, and a variety of potential remedies of which the effectiveness remains uncertain. Problem diagnosis and the search for solutions are crucial in dealing with these problems, which may be supported by the output from information systems in five ways (Visscher, 1996):

- Analysing *relationships between variables*, *e.g.* between truancy and student achievement; achievement and lesson drop out;
- Analysing *patterns over time*, *e.g.* in student intake, staff illness, truancy over several years;

- Answering *what-if questions*, *e.g.* how many students will be promoted if the promotion criteria are raised? How much money will we get if the number of students decreases by x%? How many teaching staff will be needed if x students are promoted?;
- *Policy development* based on data produced by the information system; and
- Information system-based *policy evaluation*, *e.g.* to what extent has the percentage of grade repeaters increased after the promotion criteria was adapted? Has truancy increased after the timetable was changed? What was the effect of extra mathematics lessons on student achievement?

Literature research into the factors promoting the use of school information systems for solving ill-structured management problems resulted in the selection of the following factors: perceived system quality, the perceived quality of the information the system produces (Davis & Olson, 1985; Hentschke, 1975; Stokking & Leenders, 1992); the school management attitude towards information systems (Piercy, 1987; Visscher, 1996); the extent of training; satisfaction with training; external support; internal support (Brummelhuis, 1995; Fullan, 1992; Nolan, 1996; Visscher, 1991); the number of other school policy measures to promote system usage; the degree of school consultation on resources and on educational matters; and the extent to which school management encourages system usage (Visscher, 1992).

A positive relationship was hypothesised between each of these factors on the one hand and the degree of managerial system usage on the other.

3. METHOD

In this multiple case study research, it was attempted to compare a pattern found in one case (i.e. one school) with patterns in similar and contrasting cases. The research group includes extreme cases, i.e. schools that use their information system intensively for managerial work as well as secondary schools that do not do this, or only to a small degree. The goal was to find other differences between these schools that may explain why they diverge in their extent of managerial usage. A prerequisite for inclusion was that a school uses the information system for clerical work, since clerical use is a prerequisite for managerial use. Vendors of school information systems were contacted to find schools that could be asked to participate. Those schools willing to participate were screened in an interview to determine how intensively they use the computer for clerical and managerial work. Twelve of the schools that met our criteria decided to participate, which meant that one interview was held with the principal, and one with the system manager or a clerical staff member. A prerequisite for the interview was that the interviewee uses the information system either directly or indirectly (i.e. data are obtained from colleagues). The content of the interviews was based on the literature study and was meant to determine:

- The nature and extent of managerial use; and
- The characteristics of schools with respect to the factors that possibly promote managerial use.

The draft interview was pilot-tested and adapted accordingly. Seven schools used the so-called School+ system, and five the SCHOLIS information system. The data was analysed by qualitative data analysis methods (cf. Miles & Huberman, 1984).

The interviews were audio-taped and transcribed into interview protocols. Respondents' answers were summarised and scored per variable per respondent on the basis of self-defined standards.

School scores for the variable 'extent of managerial use of a school information system' were computed by first allocating a score for the degree to which the school executes each of the five types of computer-assisted management support presented in the theoretical framework. Next, each of the five scores was transformed into the following labels and scores: 'not' (0 points), 'a little' (0.5 points), 'quite frequently' (1 point), 'much' (1.5 points), 'very much' (2 points).

For all other variables, school scores were determined by computing the average score for the two respondents of a school for a variable, and subsequently labelling the school as either 'positive', 'neutral', or 'negative' for that variable.

4. RESULTS

4.1 Extent of managerial use

Table 1 shows to what degree the research schools execute each of the five types of computer-assisted managerial support.

Table 1. The extent per school of managerial use of school information systems

School	Analyse relation-ships	Analyse patterns over time	What-if questions	Policy develop-ment	Policy evaluation	Sum score
C	V	V	V	V	V	10
D	V	V	V	V	V	10
H	V	Q	V	M	M	8
K	M	L	V	M	M	7
I	Q	Q	V	Q	Q	6
A	M	M	N	M	L	5.5
L	M	V	Q	N	L	5
F	Q	Q	N	Q	Q	4
G	Q	Q	N	Q	Q	4
E	Q	Q	N	Q	N	3
J	Q	N	N	N	N	1
B	N	N	N	N	N	0

Legend: N = not; L = a little; Q = quite frequently; M = much; V = very much

Table 1 shows that schools C and D very frequently execute all types of management support, and that managerial system use is (almost) nil in schools B and J. The twelve schools can be divided in two groups (see Table 2): six strong users (scores above 5: A, C, D, H, I, K) and six schools with little managerial usage (B, E, F, G, J, L).

The two very active managerial users know which information they need, how they can get it from the system and how to use it in policy making. They investigate a wide variety of data, the relationships between them, and develop and evaluate school policy on educational and administrative matters, informed by system information.

The other four relatively intensive users (A, H, I, K) also benefit from most of the five management activities, though with (slightly) less frequency.

In the 'little usage group', only four schools use the standard system options (standard reports on scores, absences, staff, finance, in-, through- and outflux). More complex analyses the menu does not contain are not carried out in these schools.

Almost all schools to a certain degree seem to *analyse relationships* between factors (though with varying intensity), especially with respect to student affairs (*e.g.* searching for explanations for poor student scores by studying the relationships with intake levels, truancy, lesson drop out, or the teacher). Schools that are not very active in this regard only investigate standard relationships whereas active users also analyse relationships that are not in the standard system menu.

With respect to *analysing patterns over time* the picture is similar. Some schools only use standard overviews, or do not make these analyses at all, whereas other schools make more complicated analyses, *e.g.* regarding the intake and through-put of students over time, staff absenteeism, trends in finance, etc.

The schools clearly diverge with respect to the *what-if analyses*, probably because the menus of the two information systems do not support these. Only the intensive users prove to be able to make this type of analysis, *e.g.* "How many student groups and teachers will we need in the next school year if student intake is x students?"

Schools also clearly differ in their *policy development and evaluation* activity. Some schools completely rely on human observation and judgement, others find a basis for policy development and evaluation in computer-produced data on students, finance, etc.

4.2 Factors promoting managerial use

Table 2 shows the relationships between the degree of managerial system use and other school characteristics.

Table 2. The relationship per school between the degree of managerial use and other school characteristics

Other features	Managerial use per school											
	10	10	8	7	6	5.5	5	4	4	3	1	0
	C	D	H	K	I	A	L	F	G	E	J	B
1. School management attitude	+	+	+	-	+/-	+	+/-	+/-	+	-	+	-
2. Extent of training	+	+	+	+	+	+	+/-	+	+/-	-	-	-
3. Internal support	+	+	+	+	+/-	+	+	+	+	+/-	+/-	+/-
4. Consultation on administrative matters	+	+	+	+/-	+	+	+/-	+/-	+/-	+	+/-	+/-
5. Consultation on education matters	+	+	+	+	+	+	-	+	-	+	+/-	-
6. Quality information system	-	+	-	+/-	+/-	-	+	+/-	+	-	+	+/-
7. Quality system information	+	+	+/-	+	+/-	+	+	+/-	+	+/-	+	+/-
8. Satisfaction with training	+	+/-	+/-	+	+	-	+	+/-	+/-	+/-	+/-	+
9. Promotion by school management	+	+	+/-	-	+/-	+	-	+	+	+/-	+/-	+/-
10. External support	+	+	+	+	+	+	+	+	+	+/-	+	+
11. Promoting school activities	+	+/-	+/-	+/-	+/-	+	+/-	+	+	+/-	-	+/-

The expectation that intensive users score high on the eleven selected school characteristics was confirmed for only five factors. This may imply that there is a relationship between these factors and managerial use, however, given the explorative nature of the research, that remains uncertain. Moreover, even if there is a relationship, it is questionable whether the school features cause the degree of managerial system use, or the other way around. Schools hardly differ regarding the other six factors and sometimes even have a score that is contradictory to our expectations.

4.3 School management attitude

School managers in most good practice schools are strongly convinced of the potential of the school information system and (very) motivated for its use.

Their attitude probably will positively influence the system usage activities of subordinates, and the resources allocated for system use.

Although in some of the 'bad practice schools' the school managers have a positive attitude towards system use, their opinions in some cases are not strongly supported by their management colleagues.

4.4 Extent of training

The study showed that training courses that specifically focus on managerial system usage are non-existent. In schools labelled as 'intensive users' at least one person has been trained for more than 10 (!) hours in the basic principles of system use and in programming skills (*e.g.* to retrieve information not included in the menu). Staff in other schools only have been trained for a few hours in standard system operations.

4.5 Internal support

Staff in good practice schools seem to have more system know-how. One of the staff is often experienced and supports colleagues. The six intense users also have close contacts with their system vendors (*e.g.* via user groups, or as a result of participation in a pilot group).

Although bad practice schools score quite high on this variable, some of them have difficulties in solving problems that go further than the standard problems; their system managers mainly focus on technical problems instead of promoting the use of applications.

4.6 Consultation on educational and administrative matters

Intensive users seem to consult more on educational and administrative affairs. Schools with little use speak about monthly student progress, intensive users analyse this weekly. The latter may benefit from the fact that their information systems contain valuable information on student progress and related factors.

The other six variables that were expected to have a positive relationship with system use did not to prove to differ significantly between the strong and the non-intensive system using schools.

Intensive users are more negative in their attitude towards the quality of information systems, which may be due to more experience with those systems. Lack of user friendliness in the systems is the major complaint (*e.g.* the difficulty of retrieving information not included in the menu). One cannot say that schools in general have a very positive attitude towards system quality at all.

All schools in general are satisfied or neutral with the quality of the information produced by available systems.

Both groups of schools are more or less equally (dis)satisfied with the training they have experienced. Schools that have been supported for several days by their vendor are more satisfied since this enabled the solving of many school specific problems. General, non tailor-made training courses in which school staff were burdened with information, and where there was little room for specific questions, seem to be little appreciated.

None of the schools experienced serious difficulties in finding external help (*e.g.* from a help desk) in the case of problems that could not be solved by the school itself.

Only a few schools strongly try to promote system use via school policies, *e.g.* automation policy, and the allocation of resources for information systems is very limited.

Some school managers encourage system usage by providing information, allocating resources, or compelling data entry, however the two groups of schools do not differ significantly in this respect.

Almost all good practice schools have a positive or a neutral score on 10 of the 11 factors; only their view on the quality of the information system is less positive. A considerable number of bad practice schools have a neutral or negative score for all school features. (Satisfaction with) training and the degree of consultation on administrative matters especially score neutral or negatively. External and internal support and the opinion of information system (information) quality score relatively high.

When asked for the decisive factors for successful managerial system usage, 36 factors were mentioned. Twelve concerned the quality of the information system, eight school managers' attitudes towards information systems, and six the quality of the system information.

Problems met in system usage mainly concerned (the user friendliness of) the information system and the information it produced.

5. CONCLUSION

The limitations of this explorative research are clear: the outcomes concern impressions that need to be tested in large-scale research, to justify statements about the variables as well as the interrelationships between them.

The investigation of the twelve research schools yields the following impressions. Schools vary strongly in the degree to which they benefit from the managerial support they receive from computerised information systems. Two of the schools studied frequently utilise nearly all possible types of managerial support. This also goes for four schools, however they do this less intensively. Four schools only use a number of standard options in the menu, whereas in two schools system use is almost nil.

The study of the relationship between system use and school features suggest that five factors may play an important promoting role. System use is more intense if a school is characterised by a positive attitude from school managers towards the value of information systems, more training focused on managerial use, more internal support, and more consultation on administrative and educational affairs at school level.

5.1 Recommendations

The results confirm our thoughts that convincing school managers of the relevance of information systems for the functioning of their institutions, and teaching them how to use them in school decision-making processes, is important. We need management oriented training courses that have been specifically developed and tested for this purpose.

We expect that such courses, in combination with (follow-up) support, will be of utmost importance. Motivated managers will use information systems more and encourage colleagues to do so. (For a discussion of the precise characteristics such training courses should have, see Visscher & Branderhorst (2001).)

REFERENCES

Ayres, D., Nolan, P., & Visscher, A. (1998). Computerized school information systems: Researching New Zealand use patterns and levels of use. In C. Fulmer, & P. Nolan (Eds.), *The integration of information for educational management*. Whitefield, Maine: Felicity Press.

Brummelhuis, A.C.A. ten. (1995). *Models of educational change: The introduction of computers in Dutch secondary education* (Doctoral Dissertation). Enschede: Universiteit Twente.

Davis, G.B., & Olson, M.H. (1985). *Management informatiesystemen* [Management information systems]. Schoonhoven: Academic Service.

Fullan, M.G. (1992). *Succesful school improvement: The implementation perspective and beyond.* Buckingham: Open University Press.

Hentschke, G.C. (1975). *Management operations in education.* Berkeley: McCutchan.

Miles, M.B., & Huberman, A.M. (1984). *Qualitative data analysis: A source-book of new methods.* Beverly Hills: Sage Publications.

Nolan, P. (1996). The implications of how staff handle information for the usage of school information systems. *International Journal of Educational Research, 25* (4), 323-334.

Piercy, N. (1987). *Management information systems*. London: Croom Helm.

Stokking, K.M., & Leenders, F.J. (1992). *Heeft verspreiding van informatie zin?* [Does information distribution make sense?]. Utrecht: ISOR.

Visscher, A.J. (1991). School administrative computing: A framework for analysis. *Journal of Research on Computing in Education, 24* (1), 1-19.

Visscher, A.J. (1992). *Design and evaluation of a computer-assisted management information system for secondary schools* (PhD Dissertation). Enschede: University of Twente, Department of Educational Science and Technology.

Visscher, A.J. (1996). The implications of how staff handle information for the usage of school information systems. *International Journal of Educational Research, 25* (4), 323-334.

Visscher, A.J. (1997). Facilities for computer-supported decision making in schools: Explanations for lack of use and proposals for improvement. In A.C.W. Fung, A.J. Visscher, B.Z. Barta, & D.C.B. Teather (Eds.), *Information technology in educational management for the schools of the future.* London: Chapman & Hall.

Visscher, A.J., & Bloemen, P.P.M. (1999). Evaluation and use of computer-assisted management information systems in Dutch schools. *Journal of Research on Computing in Education, 32* (1), 172-188.

Visscher, A.J., Fung, A., & Wild, P. (1999). The evaluation of the large scale implementation of a computer-assisted management information system in Hong Kong schools. *Studies in Educational Evaluation, 25*, 11-31.

Visscher, A.J., & Branderhorst, E.M. (2001). How should school managers be trained for managerial school information system usage? In P. Nolan, A. Fung, & M. Brown (Eds.), *Institutional improvement through information technology in educational management.* London: Kluwer.

8

Has a Decade of Computerisation Made a Difference in School Management?

P. Wild, D. Smith and J. Walker
Department of Education, Loughborough University, Loughborough, Leicestershire, UK LE11 3TU

Key words: School Information Systems, Longitudinal Study, Effectiveness, Usability

Abstract: The paper describes a longitudinal study to assess the effectiveness and usability of a computerised school management and administration system used in the majority of secondary schools in the UK. Case studies were made in 1990 and 1996, and in 1999 a full-scale survey was carried out in secondary schools in England. From the survey results we attempted to evaluate how successful was the system in use, and how its role has changed.

1. INTRODUCTION

Schools in the United Kingdom have experienced much organisational change over the last decade following the Education Reform Act in 1988 and the devolution of financial and managerial responsibility out of central government to schools. The government made available £325 million over three years to provide computer systems to accommodate this extra managerial load and use of these computerised systems has become increasingly important in the management of educational institutions (Visscher, 1996). Government funding was initially at 70%, with Local Education Authorities (LEAs) providing the balance. This decreased after two years to 60%, so there was a strong incentive to take up funding early on in the process. The majority of LEAs took up funding in the first year (1989). As a result many LEAs implemented new IT systems at a rapid pace. Previous studies have shown that these installations were assessed from an accountancy perspective at the expense of assessment of system usability and user acceptance (Wild *et al.*, 1992). Independent schools did not receive any funding at all from government sources.

One typical software system for computerised school management and administration used at this time was SIMS (Capita Software) which was promoted by several LEAs and already dominated the market in the early 1990's. SIMS (School Information Management System) was targeted as the system to be investigated at the start of the study when most educational establishments had only been running the software for a maximum of one year. Ten years on it is now the most widely used software of this type in England.

This paper is an investigation of how the use of this particular computer system has developed over the last decade with particular reference to its changing role as a management tool over the period. It seeks to give an overview of the situation only. A more detailed analysis of the collected data will follow at a later date.

Computerised Information Systems have been used in schools for several years, but, as with many organisational tools, it is questionable whether these systems are being used completely effectively. Studies in the Netherlands (Visscher & Bloemen, 1999) have shown that a considerable variance exists in the type and extent of Schools Information System usage. They suggest that despite the systems having evolved from a highly clerical emphasis to one supporting the activities of school managers and thereby meeting the apparent demands of the users, the wide variance in user requirements means that not all end users find them useful.

We consider that a successful computerised information system is one in which the integration of data and the related contextual and organisational information is complete. In order to achieve this it is necessary to have a comprehensive data flow underpinned by an appropriate (in education) pedagogical, organisational and managerial structure in place in the institution in question. To determine with what success this is happening in the UK, a longitudinal study was set up to assess the effectiveness and usability of SIMS as a computerised school management and administration tool. This paper describes our initial work to provide an framework on which to base assessment of how the dataflow is affected by the introduction and use of the computerised system and how this in turn has affected managerial styles and decision making within the organisation.

2. METHODOLOGY

Questionnaires were sent out to schools in England that used the SIMS information system. Sample points for the study were in 1990, 1996 and

1999 and data was obtained from questionnaires. In the first case study (1990), sixteen schools were sent two questionnaires each, one for primary (direct) and one for secondary (indirect) users. Subsequently in 1996, 31 sets of four questionnaires were returned from a sample of 78 schools and in 1999 three questionnaires were sent to each of approximately 25% of all secondary schools in England (968) with a return rate of approximately 45%. The sample of schools for this latter part of the study was taken from Local Education Authorities that were known to promote the use of SIMS, thus ensuring a high number of SIMS users responded. No attempt was made to engage the same respondent population throughout the study since this was not considered practical over such a long period of time. Data was thus obtained for a period from initial installation of SIMS (1989) over a decade of use up to 1999.

Questionnaires were sent to people who had various different roles within each school in the surveys. In the first study questionnaires were sent to direct and indirect users of SIMS. In the second survey they were sent to the Head, the SIMS Administrator, a teacher and a member of the clerical staff. In the final survey, the Head, the SIMS Administrator and a member of the clerical staff were questioned. The Head's questionnaire in both later studies included an additional section on management tasks and responsibilities relating to the use of SIMS, otherwise all questions were the same for each group of respondents.

Questions solicited information on various factors including the users' computing background and SIMS knowledge, training and support, system functionality employed, system usability and its effect on their jobs. In addition, Heads were questioned on how they used the system in support of managerial decisions. Respondents were asked in detail for their views on the system usability and were able to contribute their own comments at the end the questionnaire.

2.1 The SIMS system

SIMS is a modular system comprising various different elements. It is an integrated system in that once entered, core data is available to other modules. The producers of SIMS have tried to address the need for schools to keep accurate records whilst handling student and staff information in many different contexts, from class lists to cover rotas.

The number of modules has increased, diversified and modified since the start of our study, which coincided with the introduction of SIMS into many schools. In 1990 it was a relatively new software system and few people had much experience of using it. The earlier questionnaires reflected this in their more limited scope.

2.1.1 A brief description of SIMS modules

The current suite of modules has evolved in breadth and functionality over a period of ten years. Whilst the original modules were all DOS based, most are now available in Windows versions as well. New modules produced in the last six years are exclusively the Windows versions. The entire system is networkable and runs in either Novell or Microsoft NT environments. A degree of flexible but not cooperative working is allowed in the system in that certain modules (*e.g.* Timetabling, SENCO and Assessment Manager) can be set up as satellite systems. Thus work can proceed away from the main system (say a Deputy Head working on the timetable at home), whilst locking affected areas to prevent data editing and without affecting the rest of the system until subsequent data import from the satellite system.

The following descriptions refer to the SIMS schools suite of modules. A system designed for LEA use (SIMS EMS) holding data such as personnel records, site details, student placements and governor records links with the school system.

Use is made of alternative input devices, notably OMR (Examinations, Attendance, Options, Analyst, Assessment Suite), bar code readers (Library, Options) and links with third party software which use swipe card or remote radio linked keyboards for attendance data.

File export is possible from most modules and report generators to external packages such as spreadsheets, databases and word processors. Import of data, saved from other SIMS implementations (*e.g.* primary to secondary schools) is not well developed and in most cases impossible from the front end of the system.

Briefly, the current range of main modules is as follows:

- **Alert Manager:** Monitors data in the SIMS system and reports when critical criteria have been met. This might be used to monitor attendance records for a year group or of individual pupils or report when a department in school exceeds 80% of budget expenditure. Staff are able to set their own 'trigger points' and will be automatically notified when these are met.
- **Analyst:** Collates, analyses and presents results across a range of user-defined reviews and surveys such as opinion polls, curriculum audits and curriculum mapping. Presents results in tabular or graphical formats with a choice of filters.
- **Assessment Suite:** This suite consists of three modules that monitor and analyse pupil performance.

  Assessment Manager provides support for recording pupil marks, grades and other scores to meet school requirements for internal and National Curriculum purposes. National curriculum criteria is included with the module and updated as necessary. Users can define their own 'aspects' to record data on pupils. The system offers aggregation, mean, difference and other such facilities to analyse individual or group performance. All assessments are time and date stamped allowing historical records to be built up and measured against targets. Users can define group or individual reporting sheet layouts for, say, reporting to parents.

Assessment Analysis carries out statistical calculations on data in Assessment Manager including progression lines with residuals, predictions and targets offering comparison with externally generated progression lines for comparative purposes.

Assessment Reporter contains a number of templates which allow users to customise reports containing tables, graphics and text comments linked to grades, marks or scores stored in Assessment Manager. Multiple comment banks can be developed allowing comments to be adapted to suit the target audience.

- **Attendance:** Designed to record attendance and allow monitoring of individuals.
- **Curriculum Planner:** Designed to assist with the planning of subject matter for courses taught throughout the school. Study units are built up as the basic building blocks, each containing an outline, associated activities, programmes of study being addressed, assessment forms, necessary resources and time allocation. Once the course has been planned Curriculum Planner produces textual outlines of the course, planned outcomes in terms of attainment targets, assessment techniques and resources used.
- **Development Planner:** This module provides a structure for creating a development plan, which defines individual projects and associated tasks with details of targets and monitoring techniques.
- **Equipment Register:** Assists with the maintenance of a complete inventory of equipment in the school, facilitating stock checks, health and safety checks and audit requirements for acquisition and disposal. The module has links with the Finance module for acquisition transfer and depreciation if required.
- **Financial Management System (FMS):** A comprehensive double entry accounts package addressing general ledger, order system, accounts payable and accounts receivable. Links are provided for integration with Central Finance systems such as County Treasurers and the module links with Personnel and STAR for staff salaries and pupil billing.
- **Budget Planning:** Allows users to model budgets based on previous years or entirely new plans. Percentage increases can be applied to last

year's budget for both income and expenditure. A number of alternative plans can be developed which vary the income, expenditure and allocations to cost centres as well as exploring the effect of staffing proposals. Once approved, the chosen plan can be exported to the FMS module.

- **Key Stage Diagnostics:** Produces tables and graphs enabling schools to compare their performance in Key Stage tests and teacher assessments against national benchmarks. It can be used to identify particular strengths and weaknesses within individual pupils or groups of pupils. It is possible to define sub-groups to investigate attainment against such issues as gender. Frequency graphs and item analysis allow evaluation of test performance to be carried out, including facility indices.
- **MIDAS** (Management Information Data Access System): was designed to give easy access to information held across the SIMS system, including staff and student personal details, curriculum data, special needs, financial details, timetables, individual and school attendance statistics and statutory returns. It also includes event and conduct logs for students. The module was specifically designed for senior managers to access information easily without the need for detailed knowledge required to operate the all the individual modules holding the data.
- **Examinations:** Designed to assist with the administration of both internal and external examination seasons and sessions, the examinations modules communicate with the Examinations Boards via modem and a carrier such as British Telecom or Dialnet. Entries, amendments, forecast grades and coursework marks can be sent via modem with results, syllabus details and component details received from the Boards in the same way. OMR sheets can be printed for the input of entries and forecast grades. The module supports the nationally agreed EDI format and has comprehensive reporting and analysis functions.
- **Timetabling** Starting with a list of teachers, pupils, rooms and simple details of the timetable cycle (all imported from STAR) and first assists with the production of the curriculum plan. Several different plans can be constructed and costed before the actual timetabling process begins. This module has both manual and automatic scheduling routines and once the timetable is constructed students are assigned to the classes. Various printing and analysis routines are provided. Integral within the package is the Cover module which maintains details of teacher absence and assists with the business of assigning cover, notifying cover staff, maintaining a database of supply teachers and offering analysis functions.
- **Options:** This module facilitates the process of student options allocation, whether in a free choice or directed choice situation. Reserve

choices can also be taken in to account. Options will advise on the numbers of classes required in each subject, the block structures and will try to optimise the class sizes in keeping with the subject and ability range. The module produces various lists and analyses and exports its data for incorporation in the timetable.

- **Personnel:** The Personnel module stores personal, professional and contractual information about all teaching and non-teaching school staff. The module also links with the SIMS EMS system allowing the automatic exchange of staff information changes between a school and the Local Education Authority.
- **Photo Importer:** Allows the import of bitmap format images from whatever source – *e.g.* digital camera, scanner or video camera, and then links with the STAR or Personnel modules to import student or staff photographs for use in the SIMS modules. Many school photographic services, *e.g.* Tempest, now offer individual bitmap images for the whole school on CD ROM as part of the annual school photograph activity.
- **RepGen and RepGen Lite:** RepGen (DOS) and RepGen Lite (Windows) allow the design of individual reports from data held in the rest of the system. RepGen Lite will report across several different modules. Both modules contain pre-defined reports but users can add as many others as wished, including filters and the order of printing fields which can be stored for future use. Files can also be produced for export to other applications such as word processors or spreadsheets.
- **SENCO** (Special Educational Needs Code of Practice): This module was produced to help schools comply with the Code of Practice for the Identification and Assessment of students with Special Educational Needs. The module can hold SEN information on any pupil, including past and future reviews, special provisions, links with adults (*e.g.* educational psychologists, doctors, teachers, etc.) and Individual Education Plans. SENCO will produce a list of actions necessary in the next chosen period, automate letter production and provide status reports on outstanding correspondence.
- **STAR** (Students Teaching and Academic Record): is the main database of pupil records, holding personal, medical, historic, school and academic information on each pupil. Routines are provided for new intakes. End of year procedures and global editing features ease data entry. Photographs can be imported though Photo Importer and the system uses extracts of the Post Office post code database to ensure data accuracy with the entry of contact addresses. Modules such as Form 7 produce outputs for statutory returns based on the data held in STAR.
- **Value Added:** Used in setting targets and investigating individual and school performance based on GCSE and GCE A level data. SIMS

collects data from participating schools in August and creates benchmark statistics which can be used by schools for comparison purposes. Predicted outcomes in various subjects at A level, based on individual pupil performance at GCSE and comparison with national figures, can also be provided.

- **Visitor Log:** The Visitor Log module is designed for use in the reception area in order to maintain an accurate record of visitors. It will print personalised badges (with a photograph if linked to a digital video camera), record entry and departure times, maintain records of purpose of visits, recall previous visitor details and provide analysis functions.

3. RESULTS

3.1 Frequency of modules used

In the 1999 study, the modules most commonly used varied according to the different roles of users within the organisation (Figure 1). The scale used to measure frequency of use was as follows: everyday (100%), once a week (80%), once a month (60%), a few times a year (40%), once a year (20%), never (0%). Some modules are used to their maximum at the 20-40% level. These include Examinations, Form 7, Photo Importer, Curriculum Planner and Curriculum Modeller, Development Planner, Analyst and Value Added. It should also be noted that most of these are recent modules and although licensing agreements vary between different LEAs most end users have to pay extra for them.

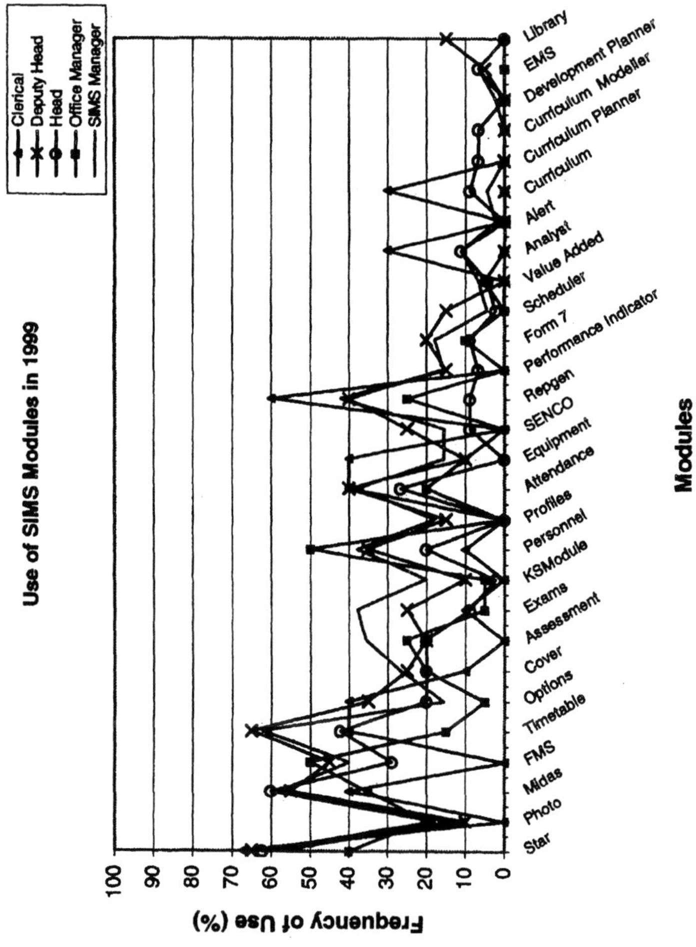

Figure 1. Frequency of SIMS module use by role (1999)

Table 1 shows overall average use of SIMS modules.

Table 1. Frequency of module use

Frequency of Use	**Valid**	**Missing**	**Median***
STAR Module	424	21	2
MIDAS Module	430	15	2
Timetabling Module	424	21	3
RepGen Module	432	13	3
Financial Management System Module	423	22	4
Examinations Module	423	22	4
Personnel Module	425	20	4
Attendance Module	419	26	4
Form 7 Module	420	25	4
Photo Importer Module	397	48	5
Options Module	407	38	5
Cover Module	413	32	5
Assessment Manager Module	414	31	5
Key Stage Diagnostics Module	404	41	5
Profiles Module	406	39	5
SENCO Module	405	40	5
Performance Indicator Module	394	51	5
Scheduler Module	390	55	5
Value Added Module	367	78	5
Analyst Module	365	80	5
Alert Manager Module	369	76	5
Curriculum Module	368	77	5
Curriculum Planner Module	370	75	5
Curriculum Modelling Module	367	78	5
Development Planner Module	365	80	5
EMS Transfer Module	364	81	5
Library Module	370	75	5
Equipment Register Module	402	43	5

*1=everyday, 2=every week, 3=every month, 4=few times a year, 5=never

The results showed that STAR had the highest overall use, particularly by Clerical and Deputy Head respondents which was to be expected since it is the core database of the SIMS system. MIDAS was the next most widely used module, this time by Deputy Heads and Heads. Alert and Development Planner were the least used modules overall.

The respondents with a clerical role in the organisation reported after STAR, the Report Generator followed by MIDAS, Timetable, Attendance and Options were the modules they used most commonly. Deputy Heads used STAR, MIDAS and Timetable (probably for planning cover) most frequently, as did SIMS Managers used who used STAR, MIDAS, Timetable and in addition, FMS. Office Managers used STAR, FMS and

Personnel; Head Teachers used STAR, MIDAS Timetable and Attendance. Some module use was unexpected. For example, according to the LEAs, 'Attendance' is run on a daily basis in every High School in Staffordshire and Derby. An overall result close to100% use could be expected. However, since use of SIMS is spread across many different people in the organisation, the people responding to the questionnaire would not necessarily have high individual use.

3.2 SIMS use in previous case studies

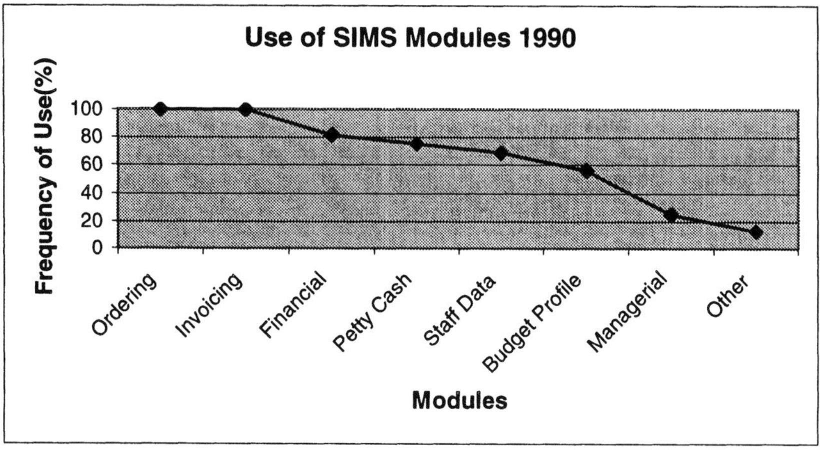

Figure 2. Direct use of SIMS modules in the 1990 case study

In 1990, the primary use of SIMS was for inventory (ordering and invoicing) and financial applications, a direct result of the delegated budget demands imposed on schools at the time. The range of modules was very limited compared to the current implementation of the software and many schools were reported as having insufficient data transferred to electromagnetic medium from hard copy to make much old data usable in the system. Problems related to job design and organisational issues were also reported as barriers to the wider use of some of the modules.

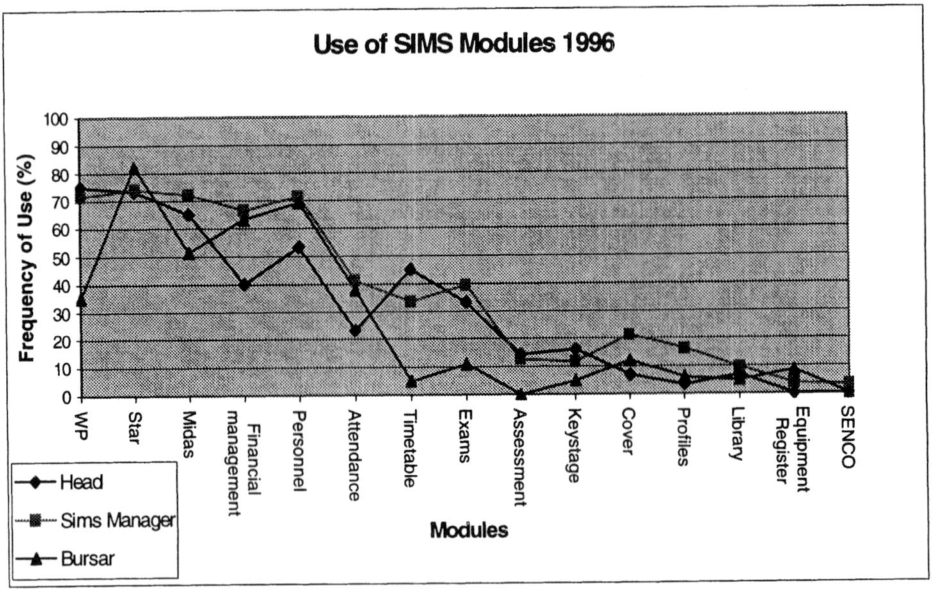

Figure 3. Direct use of SIMS modules in the 1996 case study

In this study Star, Midas and Financial Management modules are at the top of the list of frequently used modules across all users. The Head teachers used the Personnel and Timetable Modules more than the Financial Management package, which was primarily the area used by the SIMS Manager and the Bursar. The latter's use centred on Star, MIDAS, FMS and Personnel and was similar although more restricted than the usage patterns of the SIMS Manager.

The usage patterns for the modules that existed in both later studies were remarkably similar in emphasis despite the substantial increase in modules available (8 main modules in 1990, 15 in 1996, 28 in 1999), and an apparent shift in emphasis in school administration tasks over the period.

3.3 Number of hours spent per week using SIMS

In 1990 the time spent by staff working directly on SIMS rather than with its processed data was estimated at between 11-20 hours per week (see Table 2). In 1999, direct use of SIMS averaged 5-10 hours across all categories of user (see Table 3).

Table 2. Average number of hours spent using SIMS (1996)

1996	Hours per week Direct use	Hours per week Indirect use
Headteacher	1	5-10
SIMS Admin	21-30	5-10
Teacher	5-10	1-4
Bursar	>30	5-10
Average	**11-20**	**5-10**

Table 3. Average number of hours spent using SIMS (1999)

1999	Hours per week Direct use	Hours per week Indirect use
Clerical	11-20	1-4
Teacher	5-10	1
Deputy Head	1-4	1-4
Head	1	1-4
SIMS Man	5-10	1-4
Average	**5-10**	**1-4**

In the two later studies all respondents used SIMS directly while in the first study a number of head teachers did not have any hands-on system use.

The workload in terms of weekly use has clearly altered since the introduction of SIMS in 1990. It appears that the work patterns of staff involved with data processing in schools has changed and that those with a managerial role are now more involved in hands-on work with the system than at the outset of the study. The workload is more dispersed in the 1999 study, perhaps reflecting the wider use of networked systems creating greater staff access. Also likely is the wider range of modules in use supporting managerial functions resulting in broader use by school management.

3.4 Workload and stress using SIMS compared to previous systems

At the beginning of the study direct end-users were much more of the opinion that SIMS increased stress and workload. Later, when the use of computer systems in the work environment was better established and system management was more effective, users considered the workload and stress imposed by using the system was less than in earlier studies. Users' workload and stress assessments in 1996 are shown in Figure 4 and in 1999 in Figure 5.

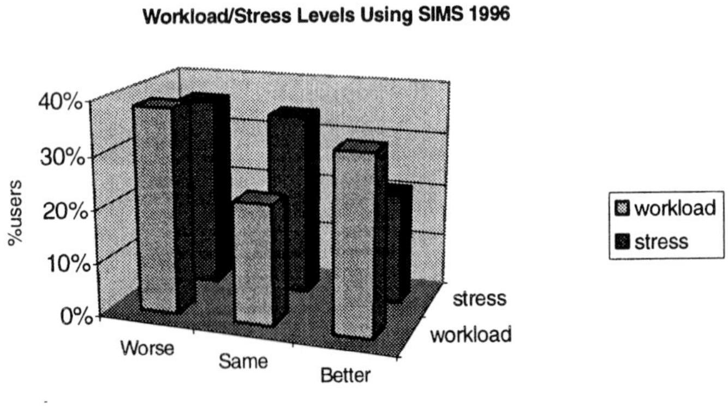

Figure 4. Workload and stress levels using SIMS (1996)

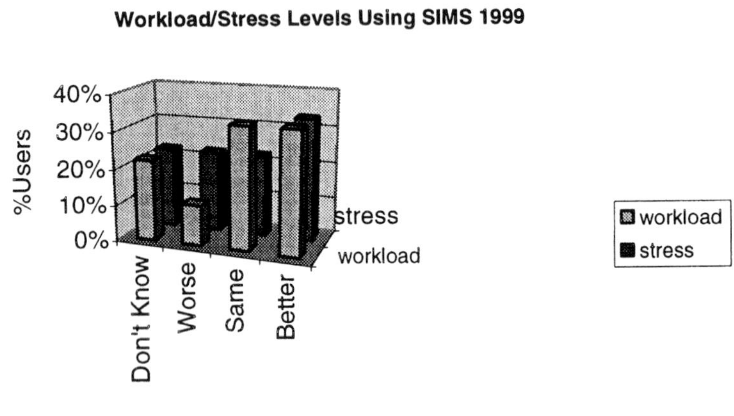

Figure 5. Workload and stress levels using SIMS (1999)

Workload was reported as lower in the 1999 study despite the fact that more data was being processed than in 1996, because the workload was dispersed among more staff, including those whose job was specifically designated as being responsible for the automated administration of the school. Stress levels have reduced probably because people are more comfortable with the computer system than in previous studies. There is a 'don't know' category in the 1999 study because some respondents had not used any other system than SIMS so could not compare workload or stress with previous systems they had used.

3.5 Modules used in making management decisions

In the 1990 study, the modules reported as being used most frequently by respondents in management were Financial Summary and Budget Profiles.

In the 1996 study, the modules most frequently cited as being used to assist in making management decisions were Star, Financial Management System, Midas, Timetable, Personnel and Attendance modules (55-89% of the sample) (see Figure 6).

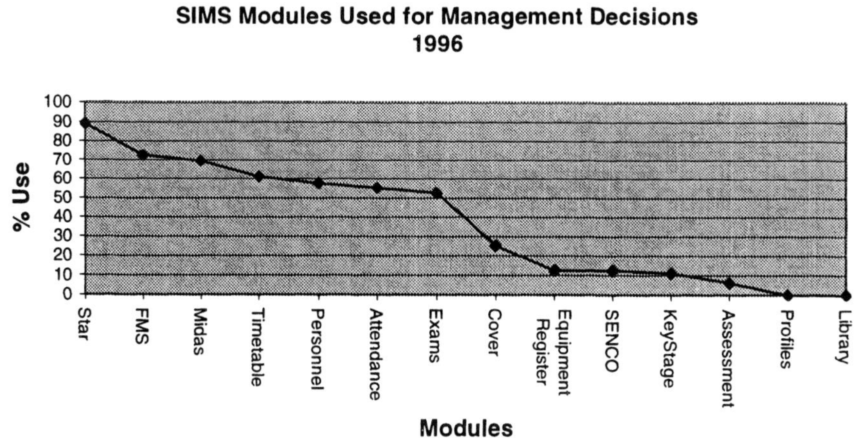

Figure 6. SIMS modules used for management decisions (1996)

In the 1999 study, the modules most commonly used as a source of management information (68-81% of the sample) used by the Head Teachers, Deputy Heads and Principals were as follows: Financial Management System (FMS), MIDAS (Data Analysis), STAR (Core system module), Timetable, Attendance and Personnel.

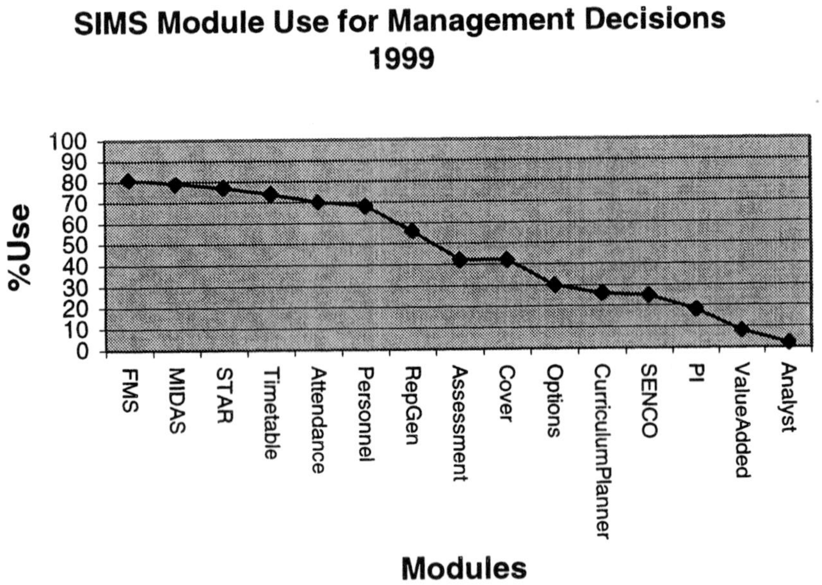

Figure 7. SIMS modules used for management decisions (1999)

The SIMS modules used in a managerial context to assist in decision-making differed from those used on a general day-to day basis by non-managerial staff. The Financial Management and MIDAS modules were the most widely used modules. STAR, Timetable, Attendance and Personnel were the next most frequently used modules. The Assessment and Cover modules were also quite frequently used in this context. An anomaly occurs in the results for the Performance Indicator Module that provides compulsory external returns for exams and attendance. When investigated further, it was found that several schools used spreadsheets such as MSExcel which were used in preference to the SIMS software module to make their returns.

The importance of Financial Management in management decision-making is still largely unchanged across the decade, but a much wider range of modules are now being employed by managers. This is probably due to the availability of additional information from new modules and the legislative pressure to consider these data.

3.6 Respondents' experience using computers

The increase in user's home computing experience was approximately 10% over the three year period from 1996-1999, and 7% at work (Table 4). There were no figures available for 1990, but we can assume that experience of using computers was lower since overall PC ownership in 1990 was much lower than in 1996. In 1998 a survey found that, in the US, 50.3% of households in the country owned a PC. The number of households buying a computer during the year rose 5.5% from 1997, figures not dissimilar to those for our UK school staff home computer use (NUA Internet Surveys, 1998).

Table 4. Experience using computers

	Home Experience	Work Experience
1996 % respondents with some or much experience	44%	55.8%
1999 % respondents with some or much experience	54.4%	62.8%

Users have clearly become more experienced and sophisticated over the decade due to their increased exposure to information technology. This has increased their expectations of all aspects of computer systems ranging from the look and feel to system functionality and task fulfilment.

3.7 System quality

Users in the 1999 study were questioned on various aspects of system quality. The majority were happy/very happy with the hardware performance compared to previous system use. According to 90% of respondents, the system usually or always worked reliably, but 70% were unhappy with their working environment, mainly due to interruptions. When asked to compare the data quality with that of the previous systems, 49% said only some/a little of the material provided by SIMS was relevant and 49% said most/all of information was relevant. Data Currency was found to be better or much better by 73%. Data Completeness was found to be better or much better by 59.8%, 8.6% found it worse and 27.7% the same.

3.8 Training in system use

In 1999 the majority of external training was by the LEAs (68%), 20% were trained directly by SIMS and the rest did not reply to the question. Internal training was received by 90% of respondents, but the duration of this training was limited (Table 5). This compared closely to the training received by respondents in the two previous case studies.

Table 5. Average hours of training (1999)

	Internal	**External**
<1hr	53%	11%
1-4hrs	28%	23%
5-10hrs	11%	19%
11-30hrs	5.9%	14%
<30hrs	2%	24%

Fifty six percent of the respondents were neutral, unhappy or very unhappy with the amount of external training. However, 63% were happy or very happy with the quality of the training they did receive.

3.9 Access to help

Getting help from within the school was found to be easy or very easy by 48% of the sample. Thirty two percent found it hard or very hard to get help outside the school from LEA or SIMS help desks.

3.10 Levels of user satisfaction

When average variable scores for levels of user satisfaction were investigated, a number fell below neutral on a 1-5 normalised scale (5 being the most positive user response, 1 the least).

In the 1999 study below neutral scores were obtained for working environment, training (internal and external), problem solving, user interface issues, comparison with previous systems (planning and communication), the amount of time spent on the system and the users' computing experience.

The amount of external training received and the quality of external training were the most significant variables in this study and showed the highest variance across user roles. Twelve other variables gave significant results, of which nine were related to user interface of the SIMS system, two to problem solving and use of help lines, and one to the effect of SIMS on school management.

In the 1990 study the differences between users' roles and their perception of the system were accentuated much more strongly. The user interface aspects of the system and comparison with previous systems used producing the lowest scores.

In 1996 comparison with previous system scores had improved and showed less significant difference between roles.

3.11 Users' comments

In 1990, the majority of direct SIMS users said that rather than saving time, SIMS wasted time because of its 'unforgiving and rigid nature'. The indirect users who all held managerial roles were much more positive about SIMS and felt that the school could not operate without a computerised administration system which they felt would become an effective management tool in the future. They mostly anticipated using the system themselves rather than relying on clerical staff to provide them with results.

In 1996 a summary of respondents' comments suggested that the biggest problem people were having was with the Report Generator module – it was too complicated and not flexible enough, making it difficult to define queries and printouts. It resulted in an inability to produce reports from various modules. The majority of users wanted a Windows environment for all modules including Report Generator.

The general feeling was that SIMS was a good system, and they had not found a better one. However, most people felt that the system needed fine tuning, that it had bugs and that they were always waiting for upgrades to sort out problems. They also said that the quality of SIMS varied greatly between modules.

In 1999 a few of the salient points that appeared in users' comments were that SIMS had made an invaluable contribution to administration efficiency. Again there were some provisos including that the cost of updating and maintaining SIMS was a problem. Some SIMS modules were not well quality controlled before shipping and SIMS needed to keep pace with developments in education and speed its updating of modules to Windows. It needed more flexibility in all modules, particularly in user assigned fields, and more presentation options, *e.g.* font styles. Report Generator was no longer a major cause of complaint since it had been rewritten for Windows.

4. CONCLUSIONS

4.1 The changing role of the information system in educational organisations

Schools have not up to now had to work under the same pressures as industry. They have always had tight budgets and different priorities from commercial organisations. It is not easy to assess cost effectiveness in an educational environment, and investment in technology was not a priority until it was forced on schools by legislation. In late 1980s, the National

Curriculum was introduced for which computer support was unavoidable. Subsequently legal requirements, such as child monitoring, Form 7 returns and external assessments, all mean that secondary schools now have to accept their commitment to IT systems to perform these tasks. At the start of our study, some schools clearly did not adopt the development ethos and were not prepared to make continuing investment in IT after the initial funding was given. Schools were not educated to spend money on technology and after the initial external investment, many just sat on the assets and made no further investment in IT. As the study progressed however, the pressure on schools to handle data effectively and produce feedback to outside agencies has steadily increased, as has the volume of data they have had to handle. This has made the use of computerised systems indispensable and forced them to change their modus operandi. In particular, pressure from UK legislative requirements detailed in the latest Government Green Paper on Education will shortly require that teachers use information such as that input into SIMS to establish pupil progress in order to assess performance related pay for teachers.

4.2 Changes in system use and perception over the decade

In the first study in 1990, the managers tended not to be the end users of the computerised systems. As in other industries at that time, they still regarded keyboarding tasks as the role of the clerical staff. Because they only used the processed data and not the system directly and were happy with the information they were getting, they did not have any objections to what was then a relatively user *un*friendly system. As the decade progressed and managerial styles changed in the educational organisation to become more devolved and by necessity more hands-on, the views of these users changed to become more discriminatory. The clerical staff still tend to be the primary users of STAR and MIDAS modules, but managerial staff and system managers are now using a wide range of modules directly. In addition there are now staff in many schools whose role is partially or wholly dedicated to the task of system management and data processing.

4.3 User requirements and system functionality

From the outset of studies of School Information Systems, it has been a criticism that commercial systems that have been developed for use in schools have fundamental problems in limited functionality and inflexibility (Wild and Fung, 1996).

In the early study the SIMS system did not map well onto the user tasks being performed manually and the users did not perceive the system as being useful. However, it appears that in both later studies, improvements to the system and increasing adaptability of users have resulted in the users' opinions of the system improving.

4.4 The survey population

In the 1990 case study it was easier to define users and non-direct users. Management did not see their role as a hands-on one in data processing. However, today as management decisions have become more devolved to a management team, as in any large organisation, it is more difficult to identify the right people to ask the appropriate questions.

It is becoming clear from the data collected that the respondents' view of SIMS is dependent on the Local Support Unit in the LEA. If the unit is effective and in particular their training programs are effective, the users' views tend to be much more positive than when the unit is of low quality. This data has yet to be analysed from the main survey.

The software is no longer novel and the users do not feel that their answers will influence the software developers in any way, particularly since the product has virtually a market monopoly in England.

4.5 Summary

The results from these studies showed an overall improvement of data handling operations in schools using SIMS. Many areas of administration have been delineated and clarified as a result of using a computerised information system. However it is one thing to have the data and another to process it effectively and use it as a source of information. The initial stages of our study suggest that these processing tools are reasonably comprehensively available in SIMS but are not necessarily being used by schools.

4.6 Further analysis

We need to consider the variables that impact on our results, including the availability of resources in different schools and whether or not the technology introduced was appropriate for the institution. We would like to define good and bad practice in management and administration using computerised school information systems such as SIMS. And we need to look at the managerial and non-managerial roles of individuals in the school organisation in more detail.

We intend that further analysis of results will provide categorisation of schools by their effectiveness as Information Handlers and will indicate why some institutions are more successful than others in this respect.

REFERENCES

Scivier, J.E. (1990). A user acceptability evaluation of a computerised administration system in secondary schools (MSc Dissertation). Loughborough: Loughborough University.

Visscher, A.J. (Ed.). (1996). Information technology in educational management. *International Journal of Educational Research, 25* (4), 289-390.

Visscher, A.J., & Bloemen, P.P.M. (1999). Evaluation and use of computer-assisted management information systems in Dutch schools. *Journal of Research on Computing in Education, 32* (1), 172-188.

Wild, P., & Fung, A. (1996). Evaluation of information technology in educational management for proactive development. *Education and Information Technologies, 1*, 239-249.

Wild, P., Scivier, J.E., & Richardson, S.J. (1992). Evaluating information technology-supported local management for schools: The user acceptability audit. *Educational Management and Administration, 20* (1), 40-48.

Department for Education and Employment. (1998). *Education Green Paper*. London: HMSO.

(1998). *PC ownership in the US*. NUA Internet Surveys, *4* (11).

9

SAMS in Hong Kong Schools: A User Acceptance Audit

A.C.W. Fung and J. Ledesma
Department of Education Studies, Hong Kong Baptist University, Renfrew Road, Kowloon, Hong Kong SAR, China
Tel: (852)-2339-5679
Fax: (852)-2794-3329
Email: alexfung@hkbu.edu.hk

Key words: Educational Management, Research, Management, Administration, Evaluation

Abstract: This paper describes how SAMS[1] has been implemented in Hong Kong schools and the degree of usage at the end of the five-year project. Through presentation of quantitative and qualitative findings, the problems faced in implementing SAMS at Hong Kong schools are discussed. The user acceptance audit reveals a low level of use and factors affecting the implementation and usage of the system are reported. Empirical evidence from the study clearly indicates the need for a client-centred approach, both in the design and implementation process, in order to be successful with computerised school information systems (SIS). The future of SAMS is also discussed.

1. INTRODUCTION

In Hong Kong, the use of information technology (IT) in education has rapidly expanded over the last two decades. In the early 1980s, computer education was introduced in secondary schools as a new subject in the curriculum. At present, almost all secondary schools offer Computer Literacy to junior form students (ages 12 to 14) and Computer Studies to senior form students (ages 15 to 16). This was further advanced, from a developmental stage to a popularisation stage, in 1993 when the Hong Kong government

[1] SAMS stands for 'School Administration and Management System', a SIS centrally developed by the Education Department of Hong Kong for all schools in the public sector.

introduced the School Administration and Management System (SAMS) – a centralised, integrated system supporting major administration and management processes, which transmitted electronic information between schools and the Education Department. The current government policy, laid down in 1997, is advocating the use of IT in support of teaching and learning across the curriculum in both primary and secondary schools.

1.1 Background of the SAMS project

In 1993, the Education Department of the Hong Kong Government initiated the use of computers in educational management on a territory-wide basis by embarking on a five-year Information Systems Strategy (ISS) aimed at improving the efficiency and effectiveness of Hong Kong education. With an investment of 70 million US dollars, an integrated computer network, linking the Education Department (ED) and all government and aided sector primary and secondary schools, was developed. Under the ISS project a centrally developed and standardised management information system, SAMS, was implemented in all schools. The SAMS consists of twelve core applications and four supporting applications. Each school in the scheme was given a local area network with four or five PC workstations to operate SAMS on the Chinese Windows platform.

1.2 The theoretical framework of the research

A review of existing literature (Bjorn-Andersen *et al.*, 1986; Fullan, 1982; Mayntz, 1984; Rogers, 1983; Stasz *et al.*, 1986) has indicated that three variable groups are important in determining the success and impact of implementing computer-assisted school information systems. These factors are: (1) features of the innovation contents, (2) features of the innovating unit, and (3) the innovation strategy used.

Drawing on the above literature, and extending Visscher's (1991) framework, a model was developed that portrays the assumed relationships between a number of variables that have bearing on the use and effects of SAMS (see Figure 1). According to Visscher *et al.* (1999), the use of SAMS is assumed to be influenced by perceived SAMS quality (block B), the features of the implementation process (block C), and of school organisations (block D). Moreover, the higher the perceived SAMS quality, the more the implementation process promotes SAMS usage; and the more the features of SAMS match the nature of schools, the more intense the use of SAMS (block E) is expected to be. Finally, the magnitude and type of use to which SAMS is put are expected to lead to both positive and negative effects (block F).

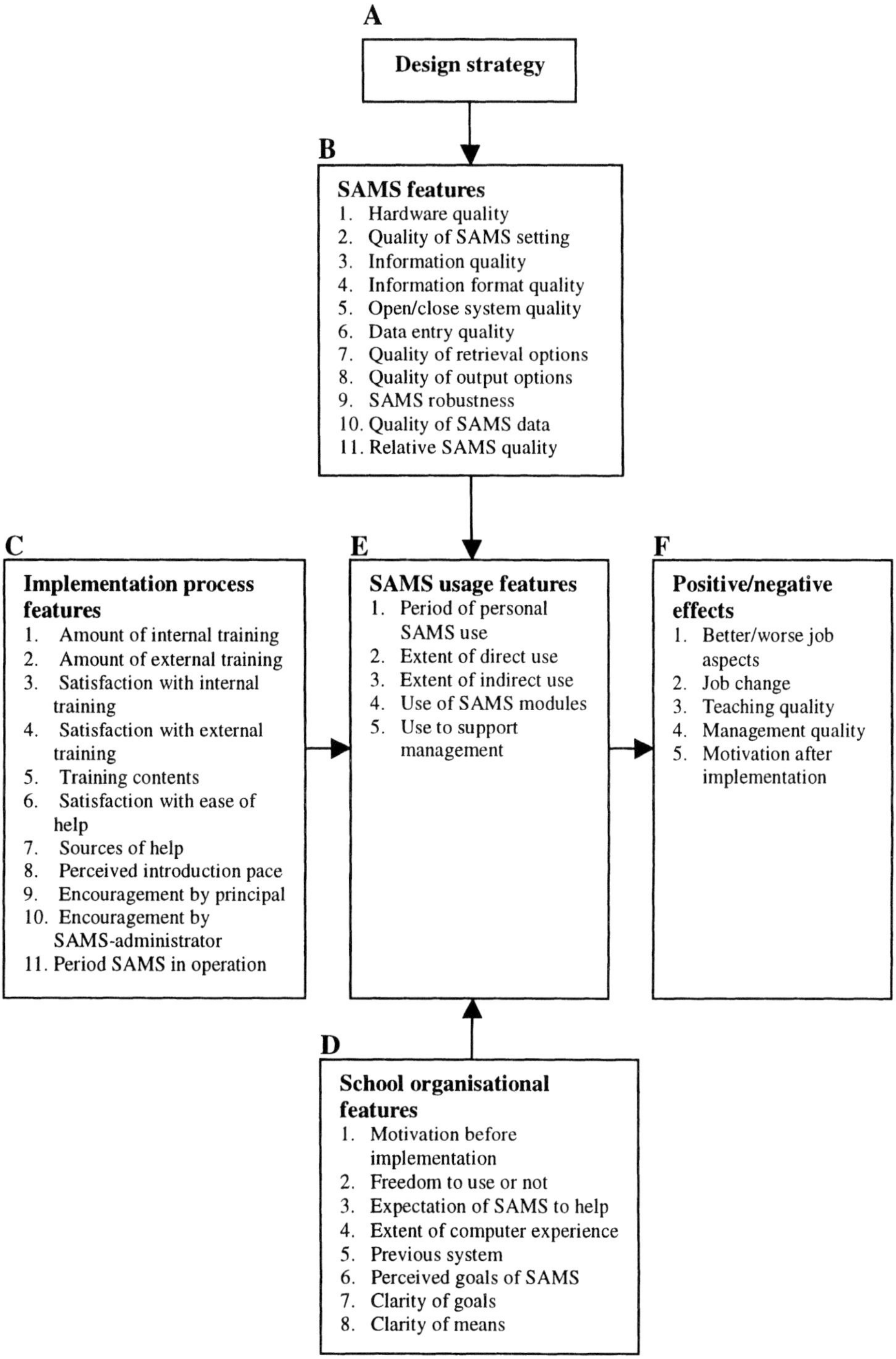

Figure 1. Variables studied and the assumed relationships between the variable groups

1.3 The research study

The comprehensive evaluation of SAMS from its commencement to completion date (1993-1998) was conducted in three phases, using both quantitative questionnaire surveys and a qualitative interview study:

1. Phase I: Quantitative Questionnaire Survey – conducted in late 1996, when SAMS had already been rolled out to half the school population, to provide an indication of the reactions and attitudes on the part of the end-users;
2. Phase II: Qualitative Interview Study – conducted in 1997; and
3. Phase III: Quantitative Questionnaire Survey – conducted in late 1998 to document the implementation status of SAMS, modes of use and degree of use over the five full project years.

A thorough discussion of results from the Phase I quantitative survey of the variables from the model has already been published (Visscher *et al.*, 1999). The present paper reports on the Phase II qualitative part of the SAMS evaluation study based on a content analysis of the comments made by the interviewees. Aspects of the interviews are used to elicit users' perceptions of using and implementing SAMS, with data from the Phase III survey included where appropriate. Lessons learnt from the Hong Kong experience, as well as the possible future of SAMS, are discussed in this paper.

2. RESEARCH METHOD

2.1 Data collection

2.1.1 Phase I quantitative data collection

By mid-November 1996, SAMS had been rolled out to 641 primary and secondary schools. Each school in this population was sent a set of four questionnaires in January 1997: one for the school principal, one for the SAMS administrator, one for a teacher (who was not the SAMS administrator), and one for a clerk/secretary. Each questionnaire consisted of forty-five common questions, while that for the school principal included six additional questions concerning school characteristics and the managerial use of SAMS. The results of that survey indicated that use of SAMS at the time was low (Visscher *et al.*, 1999).

2.1.2 Phase II qualitative data collection

In addition to the quantitative study, a series of semi-structured interviews were carried out. Three sets of interview questionnaires, incorporating significant features identified in the analyses of the survey data, were developed. Fifteen primary and fifteen secondary schools from the total 294 schools that returned the complete set of four questionnaires were then randomly selected. There were four groups of interviewees (principal, SAMS administrator, teacher, clerk) from each school. Interviews were conducted in Cantonese. Data were then transcribed and translated into English and analysed using the NUD*IST software. A NUD*IST coding tree was established reflecting the conceptual framework of the qualitative phase (Appendix 1).

The qualitative findings presented in this paper are based on the responses of 120 interviewees from 30 schools, especially the perceptions of the four user groups – principal, teacher, clerk and SAMS administrator – to the following questions:

1. What were the factors that affect (hinder or promote) SAMS usage?
2. What were the users' perceptions on the support provided for SAMS?
3. Suggestions for improvement?

2.1.3 Phase III quantitative data collection

At the end of the fifth year, in August 1998, SAMS had been rolled out to almost all primary and secondary schools. A second, shorter questionnaire was distributed to all 1265 government, private and subsidised primary, secondary and special schools. The 32-item bilingual questionnaire consisted of three sections. Section One was about the implementation of SAMS, Section Two was about IT in education in Hong Kong schools, while Section Three was about connecting the SAMS network and the IT in Education network. The questionnaire was answered by the principal or SAMS administrator on behalf of the school.

From the total school population of 1265 in Hong Kong, 961 (76%) valid questionnaires were received: 607 out of 772 from primary schools (78.6%), 306 out of 424 from secondary schools (72.2%), and 48 out of 69 from special schools (69.6%). SAMS was being used 84.5% of the primary schools, 93.5% of the secondary schools and 95.8% of the special schools.

3. FINDINGS FROM THE PHASE III SURVEY

Many studies have placed emphasis on the usefulness of IT in managing schools. In Hong Kong, the idea of using SAMS in schools has generated a wide range of responses, varying from resentment towards imposed changes to hopeful optimism about the opportunities that might exist. The study indicated a mixed response from school staff towards the use of SAMS. On one hand, users viewed the system as having design limitations and performance problems, like being "too slow... mechanistic and prescriptive". On the other hand, there was a significant positive response which saw SAMS as benefiting school management, particularly in relation to workplace requirements.

3.1 The extent of SAMS use in Hong Kong schools

The Phase III survey showed that schools did not necessarily start full operation with all modules in SAMS after the roll-out process, even though all the software modules had been installed. The amount of data input into different modules also varied from one school to another, and only a small number of schools were found to be using all the SAMS modules. In general, the degree of SAMS usage (Table 1) was shown to be on the low side. Use of SAMS by school staff was not yet widespread at the end of the five year project.

Table 1. Use of SAMS modules by schools in 1998/1999

SAMS Module in use	Primary (n=513)*	Secondary (n=286)*
School Management	448 (87.3%)	255 (89.2%)
Student	466 (90.8%)	264 (92.3%)
Student Assessment	307 (59.8%)	210 (73.4%)
Student Attendance	141 (27.5%)	118 (41.3%)
Staff	448 (87.3%)	228 (79.7%)
Staff Deployment	80 (15.6%)	78 (27.3%)
Timetabling	112 (21.8%)	144 (50.3%)
Data Management	349 (68.0%)	228 (79.7%)
Allocation	122 (23.8%)	160 (55.9%)
HKEA	9 (1.8%)	182 (63.6%)
FMP	17 (3.3%)	39 (13.6%)
Programme Scheduling	23 (4.5%)	30 (10.5%)
Special Education	2 (0.4%)	1 (0.3%)
CDS	456 (88.9%)	272 (95.1%)

* Data based on schools with SAMS installed.

3.2 Users' satisfaction with SAMS

According to the research model shown in Figure 1, use of SAMS is assumed to be influenced by the perceived SAMS quality (block B). An essential question in the survey, therefore, was to ask schools about their overall level of satisfaction with the system. The study revealed that 62.2% of the primary schools (with a mean value of 2.38 and standard deviation of 0.62), and 72.6% of the secondary schools (2.25 0.89) were satisfied with the system (Table 2).

Table 2. Overall level of satisfaction with SAMS

Level of Satisfaction	**Primary (n=513)**	**Secondary (n=286)**
[1] Very satisfactory	12 (2.3%)	11 (3.8%)
[2] Satisfactory	185 (36.1%)	153 (53.5%)
[3] Unsatisfactory	109 (21.2%)	57 (19.9%)
[4] Very Unsatisfactory	11 (2.1%)	5 (1.7%)
Total	317 (61.8%)	226 (79.0%)
Missing	196 (38.2%)	60 (21.0%)
Grand Total	513 (100.0%)	286 (100.0%)

3.3 Users' difficulties in implementing SAMS

In the Phase III survey, schools were asked to indicate the five most difficult aspects in their SAMS implementation from a list of about 20 items. Table 3 is a summary of the difficulties encountered by schools in implementing SAMS. For both primary and secondary schools, these issues are related to questions of:

- Technical manpower within the school;
- External support for troubleshooting;
- System flexibility;
- Hardware performance and adequate equipment;
- Functions not meeting school needs; and
- Training.

Table 3. Five most difficult items in SAMS implementation as perceived by schools

Primary Schools	**Secondary Schools**
Not enough technical manpower in school (67.3%)	Low hardware performance (82.5%)
Insufficient external support for troubleshooting (60.4%)	System not flexible enough (66.1%)
Low hardware performance (56.5%)	Insufficient number of workstations (49.7%)
System not flexible enough (43.3%)	SAMS functions not meeting school needs (46.2%)
Inadequate training by the ED (41.3%)	Not enough technical manpower in school (45.1%)

4. FINDINGS FROM THE QUALITATIVE INTERVIEWS

All the concerns revealed in the Phase III quantitative survey were also identified in the Phase II qualitative study. Findings from the interviews provided a deeper understanding of the factors that affect the success of a large-scale implementation of a school MIS (Management Information System) such as SAMS.

4.1 Factors that promote the use of SAMS

Variables for promoting the introduction and use of SAMS included direct motivation (i.e. the role of the Education Department and principals) and indirect motivation (i.e. self-motivation to use the system).

4.1.1 Direct motivation

Direct encouragement from the Education Department was seen as the primary factor in promoting the introduction and use of SAMS. In this regard, the ED adopted the strategy of not mailing circulars to school but instead using the communication and delivery system (CDS) function in SAMS. As a result, this is the SAMS function picked up by the largest number of schools. Another form of direct motivation seen by some schools was simply the provision of extra computers.

> "We know that if we join SAMS, we will be provided with some computers" (SAMS administrator interview, 1997).

Some staff also mentioned encouragement from the school (especially from senior people such as the principals) to use the system, as being a strong factor. To some teachers, there was pressure to use the system. They felt they were forced to use it whether they liked it or not. One teacher mentioned that the motivation to use the system depend a lot on how the principal viewed the system. If the principal thought there was a need for change, then teachers would not object. But if s/he thought that the system was useless, then the staff would also feel the same way.

> "It is very important to provide orientation to the users (teachers and clerical supports). You need to show them the advantages of using the system, such as what will be the end-product and how will they benefit from using the system" (principal interview, 1997).

4.1.2 Indirect motivation

'Acceptance by staff' was considered a factor that promoted the use of SAMS. Most respondents strongly believed that the SAMS system was a good computer system for administrative support. In fact, they had a very positive attitude towards its impact and benefits to schools. They also felt that the system could provide more systematic and accurate data storage, resulting in better quality information. One clerk remarked, "Having a systematic and organised database will not only ensure completeness of data, it will also provide convenience in retrieval of such data" (clerk interview, 1997).

Another factor was the 'ease of use' of the system. 'No increase in workload' and a 'felt need to use' the system were also equally important. As one staff commented, "We all feel that the system can help us. That is why we are very eager to use it" (clerk interview, 1997).

Some schools were lucky enough to have a computer teacher familiar with programming. 'Having the right person' who could handle the system was perceived to be important since s/he took up all the workload, thus alleviating the work of the other staff members. Most of the SAMS administrators were computer teachers, hence they have not objected to such a system. In fact, they invested a lot of their time and effort in the system management. As one clerk has mentioned, "I believe having the right person is a factor. If we don't have this person, I think we won't be able to implement the system as fast as we have done" (clerk interview, 1997).

'School expectation' was also one of the reasons for using SAMS. In fact, some schools were so computer-oriented that they were using computers in administration as early as 1988. Having a system that aligns with the direction that they want to pursue explains why these schools were keen on using SAMS. In most instances, schools were expecting SAMS to help in clerical tasks, accounts, report cards and other daily operations. Other comments provided were:

> "I think we all have a very high expectation on the system. We all hope that this system can help us manage and administer the school operations."

> "We expect the system to efficiently support us with our school management efforts."

> "We need SAMS mainly for administrative support. We hope that the system will be able to develop our school operational system."

4.2 Factors that hinder the implementation and use of SAMS

Many factors were identified as hindrances to the implementation of SAMS in schools. These include, without any order of priority: unwillingness to transfer (to abandon existing systems), staff resistance, felt need for change, school readiness, system reliability and hardware performance, system design, and system support. The following sections explain the reasons behind these factors, from the users' perspective.

4.2.1 Unwillingness to transfer (to abandon existing systems)

A prime reason for the low use of SAMS was the unwillingness of schools to abandon their current computerised system. Satisfaction was perceived to be crucial. Most staffs were satisfied with their existing system, so they felt there was no need to change to a new one (in this case, SAMS). Schools with a more familiar tailor-made computerised system of their own did not have the urge to use SAMS at all. Schools without any previous computer system tended to use SAMS more. Although the hardware and software were provided free to schools by the government, there was no policy of mandating the use of SAMS. Schools had a choice of using or not using the system. The lack of necessity and applicability of SAMS as perceived by schools has definitely hampered the degree of use.

One SAMS administrator commented that the tendency for staff members was to use their own system instead of the SAMS system since they are used to it, find it very convenient and relatively easy to use. Most importantly, they think their own system can meet their school needs and is 100% accurate and reliable.

4.2.2 Staff resistance

Some of the older teachers (the key factor being age) were quite afraid of using the computer. They were also afraid of using SAMS because they feared that they might corrupt the data. This can be explained easily by their lack of computer knowledge. In most instances, most of them were not willing or were not yet able to handle the responsibility. Resistance to using the computer was seen as an important factor. As one principal stated:

> "Younger teachers are more computer-literate than the older teachers who are not so well-equipped. The ED should try to offer more training; at the moment it is not enough. If we don't have enough training, then obviously SAMS usage will be low" (principal interview, 1997).

Perhaps it is the level of computer knowledge of staff, rather than age, that is the problem. Schools with more computer-literate teachers found it easier to promote the use of SAMS. Teachers who were familiar with computers were also more eager to take up the responsibility of SAMS administrator. They were also seen as valuable asset in troubleshooting and problem solving. Undoubtedly, teachers with less or no computer knowledge were using the system less.

The attitude of staff towards SAMS was also a contributing factor. SAMS administrators, teachers, principals or clerks who did not feel the need to use SAMS would not bother to use it at all. This lack of motivation, as well as a lack of time and a heavy workload among teachers, led to the low use of SAMS.

4.2.3 Felt need for change

In some schools where staff efficiency and staff performance (staff appraisal) were given high priority, teachers were very eager to learn since they had to come out with acceptable performance. But for some schools, staff members were not required to use SAMS; only the SAMS team members (normally a group of five teachers and clerks) handled the system. In these schools, apart from the team, no one else was using the system. Since it was not a requirement for teachers to use it, they did not make any effort to learn.

> "If the Education Department forces schools to change, then everybody will change whether they like it or not. If there is no pressure, then nothing will change even 100 years from now. Schools who are comfortable with their present system will not bother to take any action to change" (principal interview, 1997).

4.2.4 School readiness

School readiness was another factor contributing to the low degree of SAMS use. The majority of the schools were unclear on the applications and goals of SAMS. Some schools stressed that 'having the right person' was important while others mentioned that their SAMS administrator was not ready yet. Most staff members have not undertaken any training at all. Some schools were hesitant of trying for fear of corrupting their data while others lacked confidence. Some schools lacked support (manpower), resources (insufficient workstations) and facilities (space) while others did not have the time to set up the system at all.

4.2.5 System reliability and hardware performance

System reliability and system support were also seen as crucial factors. Due to frequent system breakdown, some schools started to lose faith in the system. They developed some hesitation in using the system. A couple of schools had indicated they were abandoning SAMS and reverting to their old computer system instead.

A number of system problems were reported during the interviews. For example, some schools have encountered problems with server breakdown due to 'fuse-jumping'. Others had problems with 'bugs'. The support for both hardware (by vendors) and software (by the ED) was perceived as grossly inadequate. The heavy workload and time schedule of the teachers meant they did not have the time to fix any problems or learn the system. Even if they wanted to learn, it would still affect the classes they were teaching, and so the performance of their students.

The majority of the users were disappointed with the hardware performance. None of the schools interviewed found the system speed acceptable. All the respondents commented that the system was slow, and the system configuration (server speed, insufficient RAM, small hard disk space) was not able to support the large SAMS database (especially with Chinese data entry), which led to a slow input/output response time. The system was also found by some users to be unstable. There were cases of data loss, whether due to system or operation error, and the users were unable to trace back records entered. Sometimes data mismatch also occurred ("What SAMS produces is not what we need," said one clerk). Some schools also reported a high frequency of system breakdown. One school encountered system breakdown almost once every three days. According to one teacher, "The system will come up with some unreadable fonts/silly characters. Sometimes for no reason at all, the computer operation will suddenly 'hang' (suspend)."

4.2.6 System design

There was strong agreement among interviewees that the major hindrance in the introduction and use of SAMS was the users' satisfaction with the system design. A main dissatisfaction with the system design was its 'complicated data entry method' and the system was considered inconvenient and troublesome. As one teacher remarked, "The navigation set-up is not straightforward. There are so many procedures to follow before one can proceed. That's why a lot of my colleagues find this system unattractive."

Many commented that the system lacks flexibility, while others regretted that too many upgrade versions were necessary during their implementation. Another drawback of the system design was that only a limited number of past years' records were kept on the SAMS server; the rest had to be archived onto backup diskettes or tapes. As one teacher said, "The system is very inefficient. I can't retrieve the testimonial of a student who graduated five years ago from the current workstation. I have to go back to our back-up diskettes. It is faster to check from our manual filing system. So what is the use of SAMS then?"

4.2.7 System support

According to the findings in the Phase III survey, most schools found the efficiency and quality of the support provided for SAMS to be unsatisfactory. These user perceptions are shown in Table 4.

Table 4. Level of satisfaction with the support provided

Level of Satisfaction	**Primary Schools Mean ± SD**	**Secondary Schools Mean ± SD**
EFFICIENCY		
SAMS support by the ED	2.69 ± 0.67	2.42 ± 0.81
Hardware/network support by vendor	2.58 ± 0.66	2.50 ± 0.69
QUALITY		
SAMS support by the ED	2.58 ± 0.67	2.41 ± 0.71
Hardware/network support by vendor	2.53 ± 0.63	2.39 ± 0.61

* 1 = very satisfactory, 4 = very unsatisfactory

Support for SAMS included hotline support and hardware support, as well as user manual support. The interviews provided more detailed information about these from the users' perspective.

4.2.7.1 Hotline support

The responses on the hotline support provided by the Education Department were diverse. Several schools felt the efficiency of the operator and the speed of response were acceptable. Others also commented on the willingness and dedication of the operators to help solve their problems.

To others, however, hotline support was not at all satisfactory. "The line was always engaged" was a common observation made by most users. Others experienced unanswered phone calls during office hours; some needed to wait for a long time before they got connected. When they did, operators just took down their contact details and didn't always return the calls.

One of the frustrations noted was the slow response. The waiting period was too long: responses come one month after the requests, sometimes even longer. Some information was not easily accessible; there was no provision for a prompt and correct reply. Others had to do a lot of follow-up, yet they did not get the right answers or help. Clerks mentioned that it is faster to ask the SAMS administrator or other computer teachers than to call the hotline.

Hotline operators' lack of computer knowledge was another concern for most schools. The operators did not know anything about SAMS programming; most of them were just receptionists in charge of taking messages. As a consequence, callers needed to repeat their problems at least five times before they got to the right person. Operators would refer them from one colleague to another, which was not only time consuming and frustrating but also a reflection of the inefficiency of the support provided.

> "I called up the hotline because we needed to change a setting in a certain platform. The operator doesn't know the answer so he passed me to a colleague who is also unsure of the procedures. I was told not to touch anything, make a back-up set, have it delivered to their Hong Kong office and wait for three days. The diskette came back with no changes except for one particular field. My initial reaction was that the whole process was a waste of time. Instead of sending somebody to our school to fix the system, it took them longer to work it out. I know that they are very concerned with security, but this is not an efficient way of working. If hotline support is efficient, then why bother to send somebody up to their office?" (SAMS administrator interview, 1997).

4.2.7.2 Hardware support

Not only were most users dissatisfied with the hotline support, they were also dissatisfied with the external support provided by the hardware vendor. Some interviewees considered the vendor irresponsible, hesitant and undedicated.

> "External support takes a long time to arrive at schools. We'd call them up a few times, but they are very hesitant to come. Their level of service is unacceptable. Instead of fixing the problem, they just look at the system, open an order number and tell you to wait for their next visit. When they come again, they'll give you another order number. In this way, they could charge the ED twice. But the problem still exists. They haven't solved anything" (SAMS administrator interview, 1997).

> "We are finding it inconvenient as it affects daily administrative tasks. Sometimes we can't use the system for weeks. We can't totally rely on SAMS which is why we are still keeping our old system as an alternative. If the ED can ensure in the future that the system is reliable enough, then perhaps we will consider replacing our old system" (principal interview, 1997).

4.2.7.3 User manual support

A small number of schools thought the manual was good. They liked its bilingual nature, and felt it had sufficient information and a detailed explanation of the procedures.

On the contrary, the majority of users found the manual troublesome and poorly written. It did not explain the internal structure of the system (for security reasons), and users had difficulty finding the information they needed. The content of the manual was seen to be very procedural as it only provided general information with nothing on trouble shooting.

Only a few found the booklet providing a summary of the manual useful. Most teachers found it very frustrating to read the manuals because they did not offer any suggestions. Considering their limited time and heavy workload, teachers preferred trying out the system instead of reading the manuals. As one clerk said, "You have to attend courses to understand it. You also have to use the system before you know what is being said. Overall speaking, you need time to master it."

4.2.8 SAMS training

Training is undoubtedly a crucial factor affecting the implementation and use of SAMS. When asked in the Phase III survey about the level of satisfaction with the training provided, the following feedback from users was noted (see Table 5).

Table 5. School satisfaction with the training provided

Level of Satisfaction	Primary Schools Mean ± SD	Secondary Schools Mean ± SD
Quantity of training	2.57 ± 0.64	2.20 ± 0.68
Quality of training	2.45 ± 0.60	2.31 ± 0.59
Timing of training	2.70 ± 0.71	2.33 ± 0.82
Mode of training	2.55 ± 0.65	2.21 ± 0.69

* 1 = very satisfactory, 4 = very unsatisfactory

The interviews solicited a number of positive comments related to]SAMS training, for example:

- Staff without previous knowledge of SAMS gained confidence in trying the system after attending training courses.
- Users believed that the training had helped them understand the principle or rationale of the system.
- Some users had a much increased desire to practise what they had learned.

- Others welcomed the idea of a stand-alone version since they could combine their existing data with SAMS data.
- Others were also satisfied with the trainers.

On the negative side, those dissatisfied with the quality of the training provided commented that:

- The training sessions were too fast or too slow, too detailed or too brief, frequently repetitive and superficial.
- The training courses were not tailor-made to meet the varying standards of the audiences. A teacher familiar with SAMS will find the training too simple and boring, while a novice teacher will find it difficult to comprehend.
- The sessions did not cater to individual school needs. Some believed it was too technical and not tailor-made for the individual school setting, while others found it below standard. In fact, a user commented that it was a waste of time attending the training courses.
- The trainers were unfamiliar with what they were teaching. Most of the topics were very general and taught according to the books; trainers were not able to provide an in-depth description of SAMS.
- Others found the training to be very operational, with little or no hands-on exercises. As one SAMS administrator said, "I wanted to know what happens to the data, where it goes and how I will retrieve it again. It would be good to have an idea of how the whole system functions."

There were also concerns raised about the insufficient number of training sessions and the limited trainee quota allocated to schools. The ED was seen to be putting very low priority on the training of staff, especially in allocating a quota for staff to attend training. According to some schools, even if they wanted to send more people, they were still limited by the quota allocated to them. Most respondents strongly believed that the ED should send trainers to schools for maximum benefits. Since not all teachers would have the chance to attend the training, sending trainers to schools was seen as the solution to the problem.

The timing and duration of training were seen as both unsuitable and too tight; some preferred to have intensive training for three weeks or more while others thought the duration of the workshop was too long. Others suggested having training courses on an ongoing basis, especially for new users. One SAMS administrator said:

> "There is a high yearly staff turnover. To ensure continuity in operation, training courses must be continuously provided to schools. This will also lessen the responsibility of the SAMS administrator since

> more people will know how to operate the system, hence there will be some sharing of workload" (SAMS administrator interview, 1997).

In order to fill up the limited training quota provided by the ED, while coping with the hectic teaching schedule at schools, most schools nominated different staff members to attend different SAMS training sessions. Some interviewees pointed out that such a practice of sending just anybody to attend training is unrealistic and has detrimental effects.

> "I attended a one-day workshop, which is about data entry of students' details; my other colleague attended another part of the workshop. When I attended the training, I don't actually know what was going on. I was asked to attend the training, so I went" (clerk interview, 1997).

4.3 Users' suggestions for improvement

In general, the majority of users said they accepted the philosophy of using IT in support of managing schools. To achieve such objectives with SAMS, however, improvements must be made regarding both the effectiveness of the system and the effectiveness of the support.

4.3.1 Effectiveness of the system

Respondents strongly indicated that user-friendliness and flexibility in the system were important factors for ensuring success in SAMS implementation and usage. Many users felt that there were unnecessary steps in data record entry and retrieval that could have been avoided, for example, by using a 'browse-mode' or 'form-filling' procedure. Others pointed out that the system was very tedious to use at times, as it does not have a cut/copy/paste function, and did not allow deletion of sections within a record.

As one user stated, "The whole design makes data entry and retrieval difficult. Why can't they have all the record of a particular student in one file? I have to save, exit, add, save, exit, add etc... it's very time consuming. There are too many buttons to press. I think they need to think about the whole navigation process."

Most schools indicated they would have to upgrade the system, increase the server memory and use more powerful computers to suit their needs. Some schools even showed a willingness to pay and upgrade the system by themselves, but the Education Department was not supportive of the idea as that would complicate maintenance and support for such non-standard equipment.

4.3.2 Effectiveness of the support

According to most schools, the Education Department should not assume that schools no longer need help once their teachers have joined the training courses. It is impossible to totally rely on one person (or even a team) to run SAMS. The Education Department must also ensure that the quality of the training is up to standard and expectation, and must take into consideration the time and effort demanded from the teachers.

Most schools recommended that the ED provide resources (substitution) to cover teachers on SAMS training courses; and provide an additional system supervisor at each school instead of having a teacher take up the SAMS administrator responsibility. Schools also recommended that the ED send trainers to conduct on-site training at the schools, rather than having different teachers sent to be trained in different modules at external courses.

This feedback is illustrative of the kind of improvements that school users in general expect of SAMS. In the summative evaluation of the Phase III survey, much the same result was obtained when schools were asked to identify the five areas in most need of improvement (see Table 6, percentages are schools identifying specific items of concern).

Table 6. The five areas most in need of improvement in SAMS

Primary Schools	Secondary Schools
Improve hardware performance (55.8%)	Improve hardware performance (78.7%)
Effective hotline support (52.2%)	Increase system flexibility (64.0%)
Increase system flexibility (44.6%)	More workstations (54.5%)
More training and support for add-on program development (43.7%)	Match with user requirements (50.3%)
More internal training (38.0%)	Effective hotline support (37.4%)

5. CONCLUSION

This paper has described and discussed many issues about the design and implementation of SAMS in Hong Kong schools. At the end of 1998, when the five-year project was completed, the data suggested that system use was still very limited and tended to be of an administrative rather than managerial nature in schools. The study also revealed various constraints existing in most schools that adversely affected SAMS use. A crucial element cutting across all these limiting factors appears to be the lack of a client-centred approach in both the design and implementation process. Future SIS projects can learn from the Hong Kong experience in all phases, including design, development, implementation and maintenance (training and support).

Most of the teachers interviewed believed that the introduction of information technology at the classroom or school level has the potential to substantially change their day-to-day working life. Some were of the opinion that front-line teachers should be involved in all aspects of system development since this would produce a system that would be far more likely to benefit schools, teachers and students. They also stressed that such systems must reflect and support the operating rhythms of the school, allowing more flexibility in daily operations. Unfortunately, SAMS failed to cater for such needs, as characterised by its rigid, standardised operating procedures. The large-scale implementation of SAMS has been an ambitious computerisation project. Whether schools are willing to replace their individual systems depends much on the design of SAMS and how well it is being implemented (Fung, 1996).

5.1 The future of SAMS

There is no doubt that the Education Department intended the SAMS project to improve school management effectiveness and efficiency. Irrespective of the difficulties encountered, the experience of schools with SAMS was as a building block to more successful institutional improvement through IT in educational management. Under the current government policy of integrating IT in support of teaching and learning at schools, there is the need for schools not only to better manage with IT, but also to better manage through IT.

Although the five-year project has already come to an end, it is envisaged that SAMS will not be discarded as the innovation cannot be reversed, nor can it be left stagnant as it is. On-going development is a necessity, and such development (or re-development) should be done with thought to the educational needs of the schools, as well as the technological advances of IT. As schools in Hong Kong are moving down the road of self-management according the Education Commission's ECR7 recommendation, the future SAMS would be expected to provide not only improved administrative functions, but also support for school policy and decision-making. While school improvement is being advocated under the school-based management policy, it would be reasonable to expect that the future SAMS would support school-based self-evaluation. The system designers must be prepared to adopt such a client-centred approach in order that the future SAMS truly is an administrative and management system that is welcomed by schools.

Over the past five years, technological advances have surpassed the hardware (some schools still use 486 machines) and system platform (Windows 3.1) of SAMS. In the age of the Internet, communication and connectivity is the key to success and the future SAMS will definitely have to be developed with web-based technology. Function-wise, it will also have to be developed to support the integration of teaching and learning using ICT.

In terms of sustainability, the concept of SAMS as centrally funded, developed and supported has to be re-visited. The bureaucratic model is simply not flexible enough to meet the fast changing needs of schools. Apparently some senior officials in the Information Systems Division of the ED have already recognised this and there is a likelihood that future SAMS development will be opened up to market competition. This is in line also with the decentralisation of funding to schools in the school-based management initiative. Hopefully, in the not too distant future, schools will find suites of SIS programs on the market which they can choose to meet their needs.

REFERENCES

Bjorn-Andersen, N., Eason, K., & Robey, D. (1986). *Managing computer impact.* New Jersey: Ablex.

Fullan, M. (1982). *The meaning of educational change.* New York: Teachers College Press.

Fung, A.C.W. (1997). Development of information technology in Hong Kong education over the past decade. In G. Marshall, & M. Ruohonen (Eds.), *Capacity building for IT in education in developing countries.* London: Chapman & Hall.

Hsu, S.H. (1995). Case study of the Information Systems Strategy (ISS) of the Hong Kong Education Department. In B.Z. Barta, M. Telem, & Y. Gev (Eds.), *Information technology in educational management.* London: Chapman & Hall.

Ip Tsang, B.C.H., & Lee, S.Y.F. (1996). Implementation of the School Administration and Management System: A Hong Kong experience. In A.C.W. Fung, A.J. Visscher, B.Z. Barta, & D.C.B. Teather (Eds.), *Information technology in educational management for the schools of the future.* London: Chapman & Hall.

Keen, P.G.W. (1981). Information systems and organisational change. *Communications of the ACM, 24* (1), 24-33.

Mayntz, R. (1984). Information systems and organisational effectiveness: The social perspective. In T. Bemelemans (Ed.), *Beyond productivity information systems development for organisational effectiveness.* Chichester: John Wiley.

Rogers, E.M. (1983). *Diffusion of innovations.* New York: Nichols.

Stasz, C., Bikson, T.K., & Shapiro, N.Z. (1986). *Assessing the forest service's implementation of an agencywide information system: An exploratory study.* Santa Monica, CA: Rand.

Visscher, A.J. (1991). School administrative computing: A framework for analysis. *Journal of Research on Computing in Education, 24* (1), 1-16.

Visscher, A.J. (1996). Information technology in educational management as an emerging discipline. *International Journal of Educational Research, 25* (4), 291-296.

Visscher, A.J., Fung, A.C.W., & Wild, P. (1999). The evaluation of the large scale implementation of a computer-assisted management information system in Hong Kong schools. *Studies in Educational Evaluation, 25,* 11-31.

Appendix 1

The conceptual framework of the study – NUD*IST coding tree

(1) /Base Data
- (1 1) /Base Data/School Type
  - (1 1 1) /Base Data/School Type/Catholic
  - (1 1 2) /Base Data/School Type/State
  - (1 1 3) /Base Data/School Type/Secondary
  - (1 1 4) /Base Data/School Type/Primary
  - (1 1 5) /Base Data/School Type/College
  - (1 1 6) /Base Data/School Type/Middle
  - (1 1 7) /Base Data/School Type/Tech
- (1 2) /Base Data/Respondent
  - (1 2 1) /Base Data/Respondent/Clerk
  - (1 2 2) /Base Data/Respondent/Technical Administrator
  - (1 2 3) /Base Data/Respondent/Deputy Principal
  - (1 2 4) /Base Data/Respondent/Principal

(2) /Motivation
- (2 1) /Motivation/Before
- (2 2) /Motivation/Now
- (2 3) /Motivation/Unmotivated
- (2 4) /Motivation/Motivated
- (2 5) /Motivation/Neutral
- (2 6) /Motivation/Don't Know

(3) /Open Ended Questions
- (3 1) /Open Ended Questions/First Response
- (3 2) /Open Ended Questions/Second Response
- (3 3) /Open Ended Questions/Third Response

(4) /Implementation
- (4 1) /Implementation/Encouragement
  - (4 1 1) /Implementation/Encouragement/From Principal
    - (4 1 1 1) /Implementation/Encouragement/From Principal/Yes
    - (4 1 1 2) /Implementation/Encouragement/From Principal/No
- (4 2) /Implementation/Support
  - (4 2 1) /Implementation/Support/Hot Line
  - (4 2 2) /Implementation/Support/Manuals
    - (4 2 2 1) /Implementation/Support/Manuals/Reasons
      - (4 2 2 1 1) /Implementation/Support/Manuals/Reasons/No Exercises
  - (4 2 3) /Implementation/Support/Satisfactory
  - (4 2 4) /Implementation/Support/Unsatisfactory
  - (4 2 5) /Implementation/Support/Neutral
- (4 3) /Implementation/Goals of SAMS

(4 3 1) /Implementation/Goals of SAMS/Informed
(4 3 2) /Implementation/Goals of SAMS/Not Informed
(4 3 3) /Implementation/Goals of SAMS/How
(4 3 4) /Implementation/Goals of SAMS/Your feelings
(4 3 5) /Implementation/Goals of SAMS/Clarity
(4 3 6) /Implementation/Goals of SAMS/Compatibility
(4 3 7) /Implementation/Goals of SAMS/High
(4 3 8) /Implementation/Goals of SAMS/Low
(4 4) /Implementation/Factors
(4 4 1) /Implementation/Factors/Hindered
(4 4 1 1) /Implementation/Factors/Hindered/Work Stations
(4 4 1 1 1) /Implementation/Factors/Hindered/Work Stations/Insufficient
(4 4 1 2) /Implementation/Factors/Hindered/Bugs
(4 4 2) /Implementation/Factors/Introduction
(4 4 3) /Implementation/Factors/Promoted
(4 4 3 1) /Implementation/Factors/Promoted/Computers
(4 4 3 2) /Implementation/Factors/Promoted/Directed
(4 4 3 2 1) /Implementation/Factors/Promoted/Directed/Principal
(4 4 3 2 2) /Implementation/Factors/Promoted/Directed/Ed.Dept.
(4 4 4) /Implementation/Factors/Use
(4 4 5) /Implementation/Factors/Student Information
(4 4 6) /Implementation/Factors/Student Assessment
(4 4 7) /Implementation/Factors/School Management
(4 4 8) /Implementation/Factors/ED Directive
(4 4 9) /Implementation/Factors/Staff Motivation
(4 4 10) /Implementation/Factors/Inconvenience
(4 4 11) /Implementation/Factors/Codes Password
(4 4 12) /Implementation/Factors/Incomplete System
(4 4 13) /Implementation/Factors/Convenience
(4 5) /Implementation/How
(5) /Quality
(5 1) /Quality/Ease of Use
(5 2) /Quality/Good
(5 3) /Quality/functionality
(5 3 1) /Quality/functionality/Irrelevant
(5 3 1 1) /Quality/functionality/Irrelevant/Yes
(5 3 1 2) /Quality/functionality/Irrelevant/No
(5 3 2) /Quality/functionality/Missing functionality
(5 3 3) /Quality/functionality/Navigation
(5 3 4) /Quality/functionality/Retrieval
(5 3 5) /Quality/functionality/Data Entry

(5 3 6) /Quality/functionality/Speed
(5 3 7) /Quality/functionality/Reliability
(5 3 8) /Quality/functionality/Use
(5 3 9) /Quality/functionality/School Functions
(5 3 10) /Quality/functionality/Curriculum Planning
(5 3 11) /Quality/functionality/Utilisation of Resources
(5 3 12) /Quality/functionality/Yes
(5 3 13) /Quality/functionality/No
(5 3 14) /Quality/functionality/Reasons
(5 3 14 1) /Quality/functionality/Reasons/Hardware
(5 3 15) /Quality/functionality/Improve
(5 3 16) /Quality/functionality/Not Improve
(5 3 17) /Quality/functionality/Easy
(5 3 18) /Quality/functionality/Not Easy
(5 3 19) /Quality/functionality/Responsiveness
(5 3 19 1) /Quality/functionality/Responsiveness/Hardware
(5 3 19 2) /Quality/functionality/Responsiveness/Limitations
(5 3 20) /Quality/functionality/Relevant Information
(5 3 21) /Quality/functionality/Fast
(5 3 22) /Quality/functionality/Slow
(5 4) /Quality/Not Good
(5 5) /Quality/Ease of Learning
(5 6) /Quality/Training
(5 6 1) /Quality/Training /Quality
(5 6 2) /Quality/Training /Quantity
(5 6 3) /Quality/Training /Type
(5 6 4) /Quality/Training /High
(5 6 5) /Quality/Training /Low
(5 6 6) /Quality/Training /Not Appropriate
(5 6 7) /Quality/Training /Appropriate
(5 7) /Quality/Management Support
(5 8) /Quality/Communication Links
(5 8 1) /Quality/Communication Links/HK Exam Authority
(5 8 2) /Quality/Communication Links/Educ. Dept.
(5 8 3) /Quality/Communication Links/Curriculum Development
(5 8 4) /Quality/Communication Links/Primary Schools
(5 9) /Quality/Recording
(6) /Usage
(6 1) /Usage/Users
(6 2) /Usage/Non-Users
(6 3) /Usage/Clerks
(6 4) /Usage/Reasons

(6 4 1) /Usage/Reasons/Most Important Reason
(6 4 2) /Usage/Reasons/Convenience
(6 4 2 1) /Usage/Reasons/Convenience/Convenient
(6 4 2 2) /Usage/Reasons/Convenience/Not Convenient
(6 4 3) /Usage/Reasons/Retrieval
(6 4 3 1) /Usage/Reasons/Retrieval/Need Retrieval
(6 4 3 2) /Usage/Reasons/Retrieval/Do Not Need Retrieval
(6 4 4) /Usage/Reasons/Staffing Problems
(6 4 5) /Usage/Reasons/New Versions
(6 4 6) /Usage/Reasons/Directed
(6 5) /Usage/Management
(6 5 1) /Usage/Management/Improves
(6 5 2) /Usage/Management/Does Not Improve
(6 6) /Usage/Teachers
(6 7) /Usage/SA
(6 8) /Usage/Principal
(6 9) /Usage/Time
(6 9 1) /Usage/Time/Up to Two Years
(6 9 2) /Usage/Time/Two Years or More
(6 10) /Usage/Degree of Use
(6 10 1) /Usage/Degree of Use/High
(6 10 2) /Usage/Degree of Use/Low
(6 11) /Usage/Confidence
(6 12) /Usage/High
(6 13) /Usage/Low
(6 14) /Usage/Resources
(6 14 1) /Usage/Resources/Satisfactory
(6 14 2) /Usage/Resources/Insufficient
(7) /Impact
(7 1) /Impact/Stress
(7 2) /Impact/Saves Time
(7 3) /Impact/Support
(7 4) /Impact/Increase
(7 5) /Impact/Decrease
(7 6) /Impact/Reasons
(7 7) /Impact/Yes
(7 8) /Impact/No
(7 9) /Impact/How
(7 10) /Impact/Happy
(7 11) /Impact/Unhappy
(7 12) /Impact/Workload
(8) /Own System

(8 1) /Own System/Adequate

(8 2) /Own System/Inadequate

(9) /Improve SAMS

(9 1) /Improve SAMS/First Suggestion

(9 2) /Improve SAMS/Second Suggestion

(9 3) /Improve SAMS/Third Suggestion

(9 4) /Improve SAMS/ED Provide STRN No.

(9 5) /Improve SAMS/More Personal Information

(9 6) /Improve SAMS/Communication Primary Schools

(9 7) /Improve SAMS/Better Navigation

(9 8) /Improve SAMS/Environment

(9 9) /Improve SAMS/Special Staff

(9 10) /Improve SAMS/Resources

(9 11) /Improve SAMS/Increase

(9 12) /Improve SAMS/Decrease

(9 13) /Improve SAMS/ED Support

(9 14) /Improve SAMS/Incentive

(9 15) /Improve SAMS/More Appropriate Software

(9 16) /Improve SAMS/Upgrade Hardware

(9 17) /Improve SAMS/Training

(9 18) /Improve SAMS/Speed

(9 19) /Improve SAMS/Support

10

How should School Managers be Trained for Managerial School Information System Usage?

A.J. Visscher and E.M. Branderhorst
University of Twente, Faculty of Educational Science and Technology, Department of Educational Organisation and Management

Key words: Training, School Management, Information System, Utilisation

Abstract: Although there is strong empirical evidence of the extent to and ways in which school staff have been trained for school information system usage, a solid basis for designing such training courses is lacking. In this study the literature from three disciplines of study have been analysed as a basis for systematically designing training courses. The results show that in these courses account should be taken of (1) the specific characteristics of adults and the way in which their learning activities prove to be most successful; (2) the nature of school management work; and (3) the skills, attitudes and new roles the utilisation of ICT in school management presupposes.

1. INTRODUCTION AND PROBLEM STATEMENT

Despite the fact that most secondary schools in developed countries use computer-assisted school information systems for the operation of their organisations, they tend to utilise these systems in the clerical area. Although this type of assistance is very important and most probably leads to valuable efficiency improvements, it is unacceptable that school *managerial* work receives so little support (Ayres *et al.*, 1998; Dale & Habib, 1991; Visscher, 1992; Visscher *et al.*, 1999; Visscher & Bloemen, 1999 & 2001). Management information systems not only enable the efficient execution of routine data processing work, non-routine managerial work can also increase in quality and as such improve school effectiveness.

There is also a more specific reason for attempting to increase the managerial usage of modern school information systems. The need for informed policy-making has become very important and will most probably become even stronger as schools in many countries receive more discretion to develop their own school policies. This growing school autonomy implies that schools now need to develop plans in areas where they formerly executed policies developed at national levels. Filling out this new room for policy-making requires that school staff acquire information on which they can base their plans and decisions. Computerised information systems can assist here by providing valuable management information.

There is strong empirical evidence that user training strongly influences the degree of information system usage (Fulmer, 1996; Fung, 1992; Visscher *et al.*, 1999; Visscher & Bloemen, 2001). Little is known however about the ideal contents of courses to train school managers in information system usage. The goal of this research project is to build a basis for the design of such training courses to accomplish the full utilisation of computerised school information systems at school managerial level. Its central question may be formulated as follows:

Which characteristics should a training course have, in terms of contents and instructional features, to promote the managerial usage of computer-supported school information systems successfully?

The answer is based on literature research from three different perspectives:

- The introduction of management information systems in the business sector;
- The implementation of information and communication technologies in education, especially the introduction of computer-assisted school information systems; and
- Literature on strategies for training adults.

2. RESULTS

The business sector has a much longer tradition of developing and implementing management information systems than the educational sector. The first systems for management reporting were introduced into corporations in the 1960s. Thereafter, decision support systems and so-called executive information systems were developed and installed. None of these three systems was a great success (Koers, 1993; Waal & Bulthuis, 1995). The management reporting systems proved to produce far too much data and bury managers under it. Using decision support systems required much time and specific expertise, whereas executive information systems did not prove to be the answer because of difficulties with data retrieval and the mismatch between the data produced and the data managers need. An important prerequisite for successfully introducing information systems is the development of a system that matches with the nature of managerial work in general, and the information needs of managers more specifically. At the same time the determination of these information needs proves to be very difficult (in part because managers can not indicate their needs very well) and to a certain degree undesirable because it reinforces the status quo and does not result in new types of (information) management (Ackoff, 1967; Bemelmans, 1984; Koers, 1993).

Developing performance indicators has been a popular strategy for dealing with the problem that information systems frequently spit out a lot of – too often inaccessible – information, of which the larger part is irrelevant and burdens managers instead of helping them (Baarda *et al.*, 1995; Waal & Bulthuis, 1995). An important advantage of these indicators is that their number is limited and they provide managers with information that quickly shows how the organisation functions. An interesting and not easy answerable question is which indicators would provide reliable and valid information on school organisational functioning, if one would follow the performance indicator approach.

The second source of inspiration for the design of training courses for promoting managerial system usage concerns the experience gained with introducing information and communication technology (ICT) into schools.

The literature on ICT in education is enormously wide. Many publications however contain visionary articles on the role and impact of ICT, which are in strong contrast with reality in the average school where the student-computer ratio is low (*e.g.* 65 computers in the average Dutch secondary school). Moreover, the hardware is often old and as a result does not support the modern applications. The software schools possess is often characterised by serious limitations and does not match with the existing curriculum. Although most schools have a computer network, access to the school network (*e.g.* from teachers' houses) and connections with the external world (for example the use of internet) are often a problem. In the majority of schools, a school ICT plan is lacking, and where there is one, it usually addresses the use of ICT for instruction and clerical work. Attention for managerial types of ICT usage is rare (Brummelhuis, 1998).

Visscher (1991) makes a distinction between four groups of factors influencing the impact of information system usage: the system design strategy, the resulting quality of the system, the implementation strategy, and the features of the organisation into which the system is being introduced. Since our focus is on which characteristics training courses for managers should have, we assume a given design strategy and resulting information system. What remains concerns the desirable features of the implementation process and the extent to which the various ways of system usage match with the nature of the school as an organisation (and more specifically, the match with the information needs of school managers). User training, as stated before, proves to be of utmost importance. In two large scale studies in Hong Kong and The Netherlands, a few critical success factors for information system usage have been found. In the latter study, the amount of the school's internal and external training, and the clarity of the means to accomplish the innovation, proved to be the most powerful explanations for variance in system usage. In the Hong Kong study the start motivation of users, their perception of the quality of the information the system produces, the amount of computer experience and user training, and the innovation clarity accounted for 36% of variance in information system use by clerical staff.

These results not only stress the importance of training, they also give some indications for the contents of training: try to motivate users for system usage from the start, train them to master specific computer skills, point clearly to what the training goals are, and explain which way it will be attempted to accomplish these goals. The training of school managers, if any, is usually very limited (often not more than 10 hours), too technical and too theoretical (Visscher & Bloemen, 2001).

On the other hand, early success experiences of target users participating in an innovation prove to encourage and promote implementation success strongly (Akker *et al.*, 1992). Akker *et al.* also stress that, as a start, those performing an implementation should reflect on what information system usage by school managers assumes and thereafter train users in the areas where teachers lack knowledge, skills or do not have the desired attitude. Akker *et al.* also think that examples of good system usage (including what to do with the information for organisational management), manuals and answers to FAQ are necessary for successful implementation.

Fullan *et al.* (1988) have published on the way in which IT usage by teachers may be stimulated. Because of important similarities between the problems of implementing IT for instruction and for managerial purposes, their work may be translated to our central problem. Fullan *et al.*, apart from hardware and software related matters, argue that IT instruction should teach school managers the required skills, influence their attitude in such a way that they value system usage, let them acquire the confidence that they 'can do it', and arrange that colleagues learn from each other as much as possible (multiplier strategies). Furthermore, Fullan *et al.* propose systematic and continuous support. Learned behavior should be transferred to the job. Baldwin and Ford (1988) defined this as 'positive transfer': the degree to which trainees effectively apply knowledge, skills and attitudes, gained in a training context, to their jobs. Several factors influencing transfer have been proposed by authors (Baldwin & Ford, 1988; Gielen, 1995; Seyler *et al.*, 1998). Follow-up support, the design of a training course, the trainee characteristics, as well as the organisational environment affect transfer. On the basis of the literature, the following guidelines can be formulated regarding how transfer can be promoted (Gielen, 1995; Ouden, 1992; Seyler *et al.*, 1998):

- Gain support for training from trainees, peers and supervisors;
- Conduct needs assessments as a basis for designing training courses;
- Create task similarity between training courses and work;
- Address trainee characteristics such as ability, motivation and learning style;
- Offer varied contexts and stimulate generalisation to make knowledge less context-bound;
- Trainees should have the opportunity to practice the newly learned skills in the job;
- Organise follow-up support.

What about the fit between the characteristics of school information systems and the organisational nature of schools? In the literature, schools are not portrayed as powerful policy-makers; developing school policy measures seems to be difficult, the execution of measures taken even more so (Marx, 1986).

Various types of computer-produced information can be used in school decision-making on so-called unstructured problems. Problem diagnosis and the search for solutions are crucial in dealing with these type of problems, which may be supported by the output from information systems in five ways (Visscher, 1996):

- Analysing *relationships between variables*, *e.g.* between truancy and student achievement; achievement and lesson drop out;
- Analysing *patterns over time*, *e.g.* in student intake, staff illness, truancy over several years;
- Answering *what-if questions*, *e.g.* how many students will be promoted if the promotion criteria are raised? How much money will we get if the number of students decreases by x%? How many teaching staff will be needed if x students are promoted?;
- *Policy development* based on information system produced information; and
- Information system based *policy evaluation*, *e.g.* to what extent has the percentage of grade repeaters increased after the promotion criteria were

adapted? Has truancy increased after the timetable was changed? What was the effect of extra mathematics lessons on student achievement?

School managers are not the stereotypical rational problem solver who, facing an organisational problem, carefully analyses it, generates alternative solutions and thereafter elaborates the one preferred. They prefer informal face-to-face information (including gossip and speculation) instead of formal reports containing aggregated computer data. Obtaining information quickly seems to be more important than getting high quality information.

Even if school managers are motivated for information system usage it will be a while before they achieve this. They, for instance, have to acquire new skills:

- Determining what type of information they need for their work, or for a specific problem;
- How they can get the information from their school information system;
- How it should be interpreted; and
- How it should be used in their decision-making and policy-evaluation activities (Visscher, 1996).

Too often too much and useless information is collected and processed. The fact that computers can process data very quickly may even increase this phenomenon. Selection of what is needed is therefore crucial. If this is clear, managers or their colleagues should be able to retrieve the information from the system, which may not be easy if this requires the definition of a software query.

School managers are not experienced in interpreting aggregated computer data and therefore will have to learn to determine what the data say and what is not said.

Based on the work of Romiszowski (1981), the stages in the development of the above mentioned skills can be summarised as follows:

1. Offer knowledge of what should be done, to what purpose, in what sequence and how.
2. Let them watch you do it.
3. Let them do the simple parts of the job.
4. Let them do the whole job, but observe them.
5. Put them on their own and offer a greater range of job-related application situations.

The third and last perspective for analysing the literature concerns the research on training adults. Some general characteristics of adult learners are being mentioned in the literature (Buckley, 1990; Knowles, 1978; Rogers, 1977; Thijssen & Greef, 1989):

- Participants voluntarily participate in training activities;
- Participants desire to influence the training contents and the way they will be trained, to ensure that the training matches their desires;
- The training makes use of and builds on the experiences adults have already gained; and
- There is a need for a safe environment in which experimentation is encouraged.

It is very important for trainers to bear these characteristics of adult learners in mind when preparing new materials. Above all, learners must 'own' the problem and have a positive attitude. The attitude of the school manager is critical. Unrealistic, negative attitudes may result in a lack of reception of the new learning, or even in active opposition to its use (Turnipseed & Burns, 1991). Managers have to recognise that the new learning is both relevant and necessary, and they need to be challenged by:

- A training session that immediately challenges and motivates participants;
- Training that begins with the learners' own experience and builds upon that;
- An 'open' climate, i.e. a positive environment where learning is regarded as valuable;
- Materials and methods that encourage active participation. Listening passively to others can be useful as a means of raising awareness levels, however it is seldom effective as a means of acquiring skills and changing attitudes or behaviour; and
- Opportunities for peer learning and feedback on performance.

The previous is in line with the work of Kolb (1984), an important representative of the experiential learning movement. He distinguishes between four learning phases that have to be completed to make learning useful:

- Action and real experience (what happens?);
- Observation and reflection (what happened and why did it happen?);
- Analysis and abstraction (what does it mean and what have I learnt?); and
- Modification and new action (what is going to happen next time?).

The realistic nature of the learning situation can be increased by having an experienced principal participate as an expert in dealing with a case, choosing active instructional activities, and small groups.

3. CONCLUSION

So far, neither in the business sector nor in the public sector, has managerial support by computer-assisted information systems proved to be an enormous success. There is a strong under-utilisation of the potential of information systems at that level. In the business sector this has led to the performance indicators trend: developing critical success indicators to prevent managers being buried under computer-data, and providing them with crucial information on how their organisations perform. This might be a way to operate in the school management world as well. An additional problem is that in schools decisions are often taken ad hoc; the systematic development of an explicit school-policy is rare. The full utilisation of the management support capabilities of information systems therefore requires that schools develop as organisations. School staff need to develop a number of skills:

- To recognise the value of information systems, and to develop a school information system policy;
- To determine what type of information they need for their work, or for a specific problem;
- To discover how they can get the information from their school information system;
- To learn how it should be interpreted; and
- To use it in their decision-making and policy-evaluation activities.

It is important that the training contents is in line with an analysis of what information system usage requires, in terms of attitudes, skills, and organisational roles. The probability of experiencing early success should be as great as possible. Moreover, the target users should be taught how user problems can be prevented as much as possible and how, if problems occur, they can be dealt with.

The literature on adult learning shows that successful learners have a positive attitude towards innovation and learning, and desire to achieve the learning goals. Their attitude and motivation are encouraged by clear training goals and strategy, and by examples that show the benefits of what is being learned. Training should also give them the confidence that they can master the skills.

Other factors that seem to be important for training adults:

- Involve the learners in decisions about the learning objectives, methods and materials ('ownership');
- Relate new material to what the adults already known;
- Provide experience reflection learning (real experience, reflection, abstraction and new action);
- Create a positive, open and safe learning environment with opportunities for peer learning;
- Include 'experts' in the training program;
- Provide unequivocal documentation (on paper or a FAQ page on the Internet); and
- Arrange conditions under which transfer can be enhanced, *e.g.* match with the characteristics of the trainees (motivation, ability), gain support for the training activities and organise follow-up training sessions.

The trainer should not fulfil the role of information provider, so much as operate as a coach for the learner: in co-operation with the group the trainer determines the course contents, takes account of trainees' specific situation, and coaches and stimulates them. The group should be small (*e.g.* 7-10 people), providing opportunities for all members to participate and learn from each other.

REFERENCES

Ackoff, R.L. (1967). Management MIS Information Systems. *Management Science, 14* (4).

Akker, J. van den, Keursten, P., & Plomp, T. (1992). The integration of computer use in education. *International Journal of Educational Research, 17*, 65-76.

Ayres, D., Nolan P., & Visscher, A. (1998). Computerized school information systems: Researching New Zealand use patterns and levels of use. In C. Fulmer, & P. Nolan (Eds.), *The integration of information for educational management.* Whitefield, Maine: Felicity Press.

Baarda, P.R., Kouwenhoven, C.P.M., & Werkhoven, J.A. (1995). *Ken en stuurgetallen voor personeelsmanagement* [Performance indicators for personnel management]. Deventer: Kluwer Bedrijfswetenschappen.

Bemelmans, T.M.A. (1984). *Bestuurlijke informatiesystemen en automatisering* [Administrative information systems and automation]. Leiden: H.E. Stenfert Kroese B.V.

Buckley, J. (1990). *Implementing management training in secondary schools: A guide for in-service coordinators and tutors.* London: Macmillan Education.

Brummelhuis, A.C.A. ten (1998). *ICT-monitor 1997/1998 Voortgezet onderwijs* [ICT-monitor 1997/1998 secondary education]. Enschede: Universiteit Twente, Onderzoek Centrum Toegepaste Onderwijskunde (OCTO).

Baldwin, T.T., & Ford, J.K. (1988). Transfer of training: A review and directions for future research. *Personnel Psychology, 41*, 63-105.

Dale, D.M., & Habib, A.G. (1991). Administrative computing in the Australian educational system. *Journal of Research on Computing in Education, 24* (1), 120-145.

Fullan, M.G., Miles, M.B., & Anderson, S.E. (1988). *Strategies for implementing micro computers in schools: The Ontario case.* Ontario: Ministry of Education of Ontario.

Fulmer, G.L. (1996). Training school administrators to use information systems: A review of research. *International Journal of Educational Research, 25* (4), 351-361.

Fung, A.C.W. (1992). *Management of educational innovation: The case of computer-aided administration* (PhD Thesis). London: University of London Institute of Education.

Gielen, E.W.M. (1995). *Transfer of training in a corporate setting* (Doctoral Thesis). Enschede: CopyPrint 2000.

Knowles, M.S. (1978). *The adult learner: A neglected species.* Houston: Gulf.

Koers, A.J.L. (1993). *Op het scherp van de snede: Overleven met Management Support Systems* [At daggers drawn: Surviving with management support systems]. Amsterdam: Giarte Publishing.

Kolb, D.A. (1984). *Experiential learning: Experience as the source of learning and development.* Englewood Cliffs, New Jersey: Prentice Hall.

Marx, E.C.H. (1986). Meer autonomie in het onderwijs: Een ontwikkelingsmodel [More autonomy: A developmental model]. *Vrijspraak,* 9.

Ouden, M.D. den (1992). *Transfer na bedrijfsopleidingen: Een veldonderzoek naar de voornemens, sociale voornemens, sociale normen, beheersing en sociale steun bij opleidingstransfer* [Transfer of corporate training: A field study on the role of (social) plans, social norms, control and support in the transfer of training] (Doctoral Thesis). Amsterdam: Thesis Publishers.

Rogers, J. (1977). *Adults learning.* Milton Keynes: Open University Press.

Romiszowski, A.J. (1981). *Designing instructional systems. Decision making in course planning and curriculum design.* Londen: Kogan Page.

Seyler, D.L., Holton III, E.F., Bates, R.A., Burnett, M.F., & Carvalho, M.A. (1998). Factors affecting motivation to transfer training. *International Journal of Training and Development,* 2 (1), 2-16.

Thijssen, J.G.L., & Greef, I. de. (1989). Het leren van volwassenen: Theorieën en grondprincipes [How adults learn: Theories and basic principles]. In J.W.M. Kessels, & C.A. Smit (Eds.), *Handboek opleiders in organisaties.* Deventer: Kluwer Bedrijfswetenschappen.

Turnipseed, D.L., & Burns, O.M. (1991). Contemporary attitudes toward computers: An explanation of behavior. *Journal of Research on Computing in Education,* 23(4), 611-625.

Visscher, A.J. (1991). School administrative computing: A framework for analysis. *Journal of Research on Computing in Education, 24* (1), 1-19.

Visscher, A.J. (1992). *Design and evaluation of a computer-assisted management information system for secondary schools* (PhD Dissertation). Enschede: University of Twente, Department of Educational Science and Technology.

Visscher, A.J. (1996). The implications of how staff handle information for the usage of school information systems. *International Journal of Educational Research, 25* (4), 323-334.

Visscher, A.J., & Bloemen, P.P.M. (1999). Evaluation and use of computer-assisted management information systems in Dutch schools. *Journal of Research on Computing in Education, 32* (1), 172-188.

Visscher, A.J., & Bloemen, P.P.M. (2001). School managerial usage of computer-assisted school information systems: A comparison of good practice and bad practice schools. In P. Nolan, & A. Fung (Eds.), *Institutional improvement through information technology in educational management.* London: Kluwer.

Visscher, A.J., Fung, A., & Wild, P. (1999). The evaluation of the large scale implementation of a computer-assisted management information system in Hong Kong schools. *Studies in Educational Evaluation, 25*, 11-31.

Waal, A.A. de, & Bulthuis, H. (1995). *Cijfers zeggen niet* alles [Figures do not tell you everything]. Deventer: Kluwer Bedrijfswetenschappen.

11

Supporting UK Teachers through the National Grid for Learning

I. Selwood[1], D. Smith[2] and J. Wisehart[2]
[1]*The University of Birmingham, School of Education, Edgbaston, Birmingham, UK.*
Email: I.D.Selwood@Bham.AC.UK
[2]*Loughborough University, Department of Education, Loughborough, UK.*

Keywords: Education, Teachers, Administration, Management, Internet

Abstract: In 1997 the "New Labour Party" came to power in the UK. Since their election they have announced spending of over one billion pounds on Information and Communications Technology (ICT) in Education. Most of this investment centres on the National Grid for Learning (NGfL). Two years after NGfL's launch, this paper examines the background to, and introduction of, the NGfL in the UK, and how this investment will support school teachers. The paper tends to focus on how teachers might use the NGfL to relieve their administrative burden, rather than the features of the NGfL that might be used in the classroom to teach pupils and aid their learning. The paper also reports on teachers' initial reactions to the opportunities provided for electronic communications.

1. INTRODUCTION

Comparatively little has been written about how Information and Communications Technology (ICT) can support classroom teachers in improving their own professional efficiency and reducing their administrative and bureaucratic burdens. However, in response to the UK Government's Green Paper "Teachers: Meeting the Challenge of Change" (DfEE 1998) one of the strongest views from 41,000 responses was the potential of ICT to reduce teachers' administrative burdens (Becta, 1999). Addressing this issue in terms of the intended outcomes of training teachers in ICT, the Teacher Training Agency (TTA, 1998a) notes that teachers should be using ICT for:

- Administration, record-keeping, analysis, reporting, and transfer of information;
- To join professional discussions, locate and access teaching plans, material and other sources of help through the National Grid for Learning (NGfL); and
- To support their continuing professional development.

Whilst the prime purpose of the NGfL is not to support teachers in the areas noted, it undoubtedly has the potential to do so. This paper will examine how the NGfL in the UK has developed and how in particular it can be used to support classroom teachers in some of the areas detailed above. However, due to the nature of the topic and the fact that many classroom teachers have or will progress to managerial roles, other areas such as using ICT to support teaching and learning and the use of ICT to support educational management will be touched upon.

2. BACKGROUND

The idea of supporting teachers on-line is not new. Since the early 1980s telecommunications have been used to provide schools with on-line educational databases to support teaching, learning and administration. Administration in this context is taken to cover not only administration of the school but the day-to-day administration that classroom teachers are expected to do, such as planning schemes of work and lessons. In his paper "Successfully Establishing a 'National Grid for Learning': Have we been here before?" Selwyn (1999) discusses some of the early remote electronic information systems (Prestel Education, TTNS (later Campus 2000) and NERIS) used in the UK. Many of the resources available on these systems were of undoubted value. However, the cost of subscribing and communicating with them and the technology of the day, a modem connected to at best one early PC, meant that uptake and usage of all three systems were limited. Also, technological developments, including the rapid development of the Internet in the early 1990s, sounded the death knell of these early systems.

In 1995, speaking at the British Education Training and Technology Exhibition, the then Secretary of State for Education invited industry and the education community to work together to develop a commonly accessible national - and ultimately international - education superhighway (DfE, 1995). After initial consultation, the Government published a policy paper and launched the Education Departments' Superhighways Initiative (EDSI) (DfEE, 1995). EDSI involved 25 pilot projects and related initiatives involving more than 1000 schools of all types and phases. The schools involved used ICT for a wide variety of purposes including electronic communication (fax, email, text-based and video conferencing), and accessing and creating resources on the Internet. The evaluation findings of EDSI (DfEE, 1997) reported benefits including: improved subject learning across a broad range of subjects and ages; increased differentiation, shift towards project work and a more integrated curriculum; the development of network literacy; improved motivation, attitudes and self-esteem; the development of independent learning, research skills, creative thinking and problem solving; and social development and peer tutoring. However, a word of caution should be included here as the results of such "experiments" with learners may be influenced by the novelty factor. Less likely to be influenced by novelty factors and more central to this paper are the four key benefits for using ICT in management and administration reported in EDSI evaluation. These are:

- Reduced administrative communications costs for schools when contacting other schools, exam boards, local and central Government departments;
- Easier communications in such matters as pupil transfer and liaison on pupils with special needs, and supporting curriculum continuity between phases;
- Teachers able to access the school electronically from home for record keeping, school reports, exam administration; and
- Training in educational management and administration can be cheaper and enhanced by saving on travel and cover costs.

EDSI undoubtedly influenced what was to follow. However, an election was imminent in the UK and the then opposition, "New Labour", were campaigning on a platform of improving education. Central to this was their belief in the value of ICT in supporting teaching and learning. In 1995, Tony Blair had promised that if elected, all schools would be connected to the Internet. New Labour also commissioned an independent enquiry into the state of ICT in schools (Stevenson, 1997) informed by a survey "The Future of Information Technology in UK Schools" carried out by McKinsey and Company (1997). The inquiry concluded that the state of ICT in UK schools was primitive and not improving and that it should be a national priority to increase the use of ICT in schools. Stevenson also introduced the concept of an external ICT network to be set up to enable teachers to learn from each other.

Following its election in 1997, the "New Labour" Government introduced a proposal for such a network: the National Grid for Learning, in its consultation paper "Connecting the Learning Society" (DfEE, 1997b). This can be seen as a direct response to Stevenson's recommendations. In it the Government outlined its targets for ICT in Education, many of which revolve around the setting up of the NGfL.

3. THE NATIONAL GRID FOR LEARNING (NGfL)

The NGfL was visualised as:

> "A mosaic of inter-connecting networks and education services based on the Internet which will support teaching, learning, training and administration in schools, colleges, universities, libraries, the workplace and homes" (DfEE, 1997b:3).

Thus the NGfL was envisaged as supporting all kinds of learners and teachers at all levels, though schools and their teachers were to be the initial focus. The NGfL is conceptualised not just as a website but as an Internet-based on-line communications network linking schools, colleges, higher education, libraries and museums to other education services and web sites. These include government funded virtual teachers' centres for England, Northern Ireland, Scotland and Wales (see Appendix 1), LEA sites and Intranets, school sites and industry funded sites. Many sites allow and will continue to allow free access, although some sites will require subscriptions or payment. Moreover, the NGfL is seen as having three components, infrastructure, content and practice (Becta, 1999).

3.1 Infrastructure

It is government policy that by 2002 all schools will be on the NGfL/Internet. To achieve this, £700 million of government funding has been made available to set up access to the Internet (normally ISDN2 or Leased Line), create the infrastructure in schools and replace obsolete hardware. The first schools have received funding and are now connected.

Other aspects of the NGfL, such as setting up 700 ICT learning centres and developing community grids for learning based on public libraries, are also funded but are outside the scope of this paper. The Government is also trying to ensure that telecommunications costs in general, and for schools in particular, will fall. Additionally, the Government has established a system of NGfL Certified Managed Services. Certified (approved) providers will supply educational institutions with a local area network of computers, cabling infrastructure, Internet access, technical support and training (NGfL, 1999).

3.2 Content

The Government's aims are ambitious with regard to content. They would like the UK to become a centre of excellence in the development of networked software content for education and lifelong learning and become a major exporter of learning services. To achieve this aim, £50 million is available to create content to support life long learning. Schools and LEAs are also encouraged to develop content and make it available over the NGfL.

3.3 Practice

For the NGfL to be a success (i.e. to improve education), teachers must be confident and competent in their use of ICT, and this is another of the Government's targets. Stevenson (1997) highlighted the need for training teachers in ICT, and this was supported by statistics produced by the Department for Education and Employment (DfEE) (1999). Two initiatives were introduced to meet this need. From September 1998, a National Curriculum for ICT (TTA, 1998b) in teacher education became a mandatory part of initial teacher training. In the (northern) summer of 1999, a £230 million, lottery funded (New Opportunities Fund (NOF)) scheme to provide training or re-training for all 500,000 practising teachers and school librarians began, again to be completed by 2002. The curriculum for initial teacher training and the expected outcomes of the NOF training (TTA, 1998a) are, as one would expect, extremely similar. Though the focus of these two schemes is on developing teacher competence in "The Use of Information and Communications Technology in Subject Teaching", administration and management are not ignored. Outcomes in the NOF document include:

> "can employ common ICT tools for their own and pupils' benefit, ...and can use a range of ICT resources, at the level of general users *rather than network...managers*" (TTA, 1998a: 9); and
>
> "Teachers should know how to use ICT to improve their own professional efficiency and to reduce administrative and bureaucratic burdens..." (TTA, 1998a:13).

The final target that must be mentioned in this section is the Government's wish to see general administrative communications to schools, by the UK Education Departments, Ofsted, and non-departmental public bodies, and the collection of data from schools, cease to be paper based by 2002 (Becta, 1998). This target has subsequently been modified and quantified - 25% of communications from DfEE to schools are to be electronic by 2002 (Becta, 1999).

The most recent government initiative, only announced as this paper was being prepared, that will undoubtedly encourage teachers to use ICT, is the "Computers for Teachers Initiative" (NGfL, 2000). Computers for Teachers is a three year, £20 million initiative to assist teachers to buy their own computer by offering a subsidy of up to £500 per person. The subsidy will cover up to half the cost of specified packages and will include free Internet access.

3.4 The NGfL site (http://www.ngfl.gov.uk/ngfl/index.html)

The home page of the NGfL site provides links to its various sub-sections: Schools, FE, HE, Lifelong Learning and University For Industry, Career Development, Libraries, Museums and Galleries, Community Grids, International Links, Government and Agencies, and the Learning Resource Index (LRI). Most of these areas do not directly concern schools. Nevertheless, their content may well interest teachers of particular subjects, for example History and Art teachers would find 'Museums and Galleries' useful. Following the 'Schools' link takes users to a somewhat disappointing set of links: the four VTCs; the standards site; governor, parent and special needs centres; Maths Year 2000; Managed Services; and Computers for Teachers. There is no link to Becta, who maintain the NGfL and have their own useful site; this link has to be found elsewhere.

3.5 Virtual Teachers' Centre (VTC)

The main initial focus of the NGfL was originally seen as the creation of a Virtual Teachers' Centre (VTC) (DfEE, 1997b), and this is probably the area that should help teachers most in the area of administration. The reality is that four VTCs have been created (Appendix 1), each of which serves their own area of the UK, though it is obviously possible to access all of them. Each VTC has a different structure and contents, though there are strong similarities between the English and Welsh VTCs. What follows is a brief overview of the English VTC - henceforth VTC. Becta (The British Educational Communications and Technology Agency) manages the VTC for the DfEE. The VTC can be searched by subject (curriculum area), search engine or site map. There are currently six major areas.

1. **Reception** – contains news, copyright, and feedback about the site.
2. **Library** – the library at present mainly contains links to other sites, such as Education Departments and Educational Agencies, information about current projects, and various publications.
3. **Meeting Room** – is designed to act as a starting of point to join various educational forums. Links are provided to many web-based discussion groups (conferences) and details of how to join mailing lists are given.
4. **Classroom Resources** – links at the top of this page lead to: 1000 independent reviews of CD-ROMs; Supporting the Curriculum with ICT, which contains resources developed under the DfEE-funded curriculum IT support projects (and can be searched by subject), and web site reviews; the LRI, which is discussed later; and an Educational Software database. There are also areas for Primary, Secondary, Special Needs and Careers.
5. **School Management** – this area has far more options than any other area. Initially it is divided into sub-groups entitled: Effective Management and Leadership, Financial Resource Management, Data Collection and Information Management, National Curriculum and Raising Standards, School Policies and Procedures, Consultations, and Other Publications. Click on any of these and you are presented with a wealth of further links to sites and documents within those sites. This section certainly appears to be comprehensive when it comes to official publications from the DfEE and other educational agencies concerning all aspects of school education.
6. **Professional Development** – contains support materials from several projects to help teachers enhance their use of ICT; information about and links to PD providers, though these are limited to ICT, including those approved under the NOF training scheme and the TTA; links to subject and professional associations; and, strangely, some links to various sources of classroom materials.

It is apparent when examining the range of facilities offered in the VTC that, with the addition of an email facility, most of the uses of ICT raised in the introduction are available through the VTC. However, the depth and breadth of coverage are open to question, and if this were the only site available to teachers there would be cause for concern.

3.6 Learning Resource Index (LRI) (http://www.ngfl.gov.uk/ngfl/lri/index.html)

This is potentially a very valuable resource for classroom teachers as it should save time in finding resources and planning lessons. However, the

LRI does cover all phases of education so its use will be wider. In many ways its aims are similar to its predecessor NERIS, but is far more ambitious in that it gives NGfL users a ready means of locating sites and resources that are on the Grid. The NGfL also includes links to many educational sites, which lie beyond the Grid itself, and references non-Internet educational resources and support. The rules governing entries to the LRI are stringent and should help to guarantee quality. The search mechanism is effective and simple to use.

3.7 Becta (http://www.becta.org.uk/)

Becta (British Educational Communications and Technology Agency) is a Government funded agency "...who work to ensure that ICT supports the Government's efforts to drive up standards..." (Becta, 2000). Becta also maintains the three sites thus far discussed. Since its inception, the Becta site has always been one of the first places for UK teachers to look for help on all aspects of the use of ICT in education. The site was re-launched in January 2000 and now consists of nine main areas – About Becta; News and Comment, including key educational documents; Publications; Schools; Lifelong Learning and FE; Support Providers; Inclusion; International Activities; and Technology Advice and Information. This last area contains many useful information sheets concerning ICT, but unfortunately no longer contains all the school subject information sheets it used to. Mailing lists and forums also exist on the site but users must register for these. Whilst many of the areas mentioned briefly above have implications for administration, the 'Schools' area now contains the 'Senior Managers in Schools' section (http://www.becta.org.uk/schools/smanagers/index.html). This has subsections on ICT policy and planning, Senior Managers' Conference, NPQH (National Professional Qualification for Headship), Training Providers, News, and Managing with ICT.

The sites detailed above (in Sections 3.4, 3.5 and 3.6) are the probably the main sites on the NGfL, but according to Becta in October 1999 the NGfL contained 250,000 documents from 250 sites (Becta, 1999). Many of these contain information that support teachers in the sort of administrative activities noted in the introduction, and have the sort of benefits highlighted in EDSI evaluation (DfEE, 1997). The sites are there and growing, but are teachers using them?

4. TEACHERS' INITIAL RESPONSES TO THE NGfL

The implementation of the infrastructure for NGfL has been broken down into yearly phases. What follows are some of the results of a survey carried out in a Midlands LEA at the end of the initial hardware installation to provide or enhance Internet access in approximately a third of their schools. Questionnaires were sent to 98 schools and 51 (8 secondary and 43 primary were returned (52%). The answers to the following questions are of interest.

4.1 Are you satisfied with the equipment and software nowit's installed?

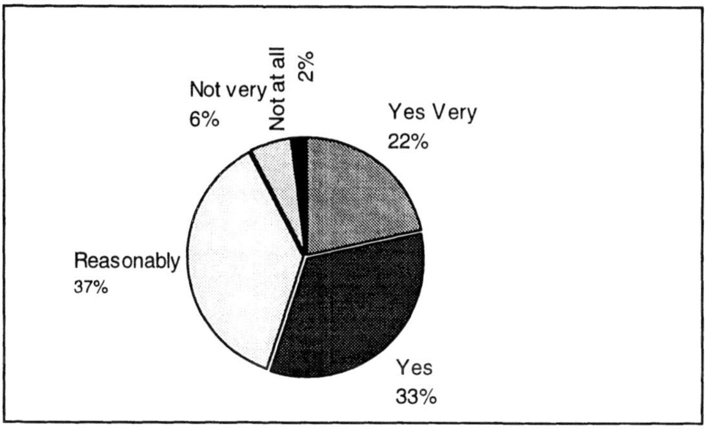

Figure 1. Satisfaction with equipment and software

The majority of the respondents were satisfied or very satisfied with the equipment and software once it was installed. Twenty-seven of the schools commented on the completed installation. Some hardware was causing problems, and hardware fault reports accounted for 19% of comments. A number had problems with software installation and set-up (15%). The company doing the installation was also criticised (19% of comments) for having a not very helpful 'Helpline' and manuals that were 'a bit vague'. However, one respondent commended the support materials and another was pleased that having the new equipment encouraged staff use of the Internet.

4.2 Do many staff use the Internet?

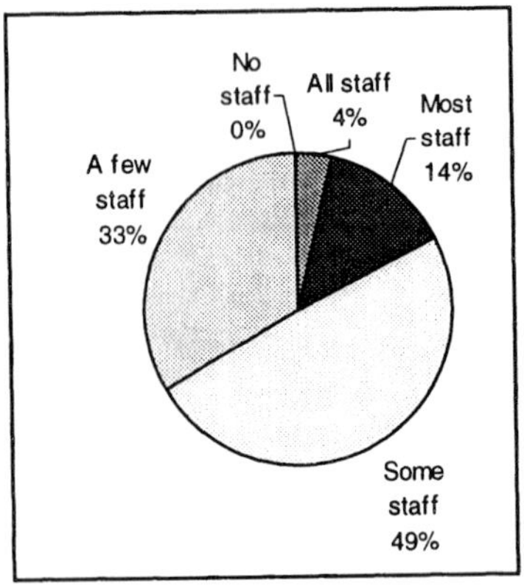

Figure 2. Staff use of the Internet

In every school in the sample at least some staff had tried using the Internet. However, only 4% said that all staff in the school used it.

4.3 Do staff feel confident that they can access useful material on the Internet?

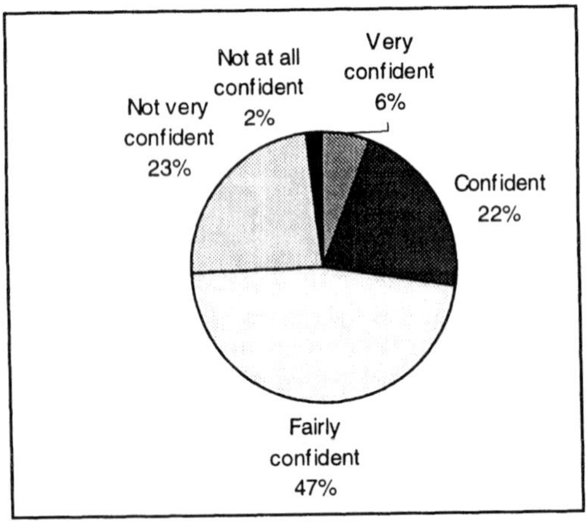

Figure 3. Confidence in accessing the Internet

The majority of staff in schools were fairly confident, confident or very confident about using the Internet.

4.4 Do staff use email?

Table 1. Staff email use

Used in school	Percent	Used outside school	Percent
Yes	34.7	Yes	75.5
No	65.3	No	24.5

Over three quarters of the schools said that staff used email outside school but only 34.7% used it internally at school.

4.5 Which staff regularly use the WWW in school?

A wide range of responses was obtained from this question. The only consistent information was that most schools used the World Wide Web, though 16% of the schools reported that staff did not use the WWW or did not use it regularly. Only 10% claimed that most or all their staff used it regularly. One respondent said that parents also used the web regularly in school.

5. CONCLUSION

This paper has examined the background to, and introduction of, the NGfL and the aspects of it that should support classroom teachers in their work.

The results of the Midlands survey show that even at the early stages of implementation, teachers are using the Internet, the WWW and Email, and are confident in their use – though there is scope for far greater and more regular use. Though the survey focused on schools' connection to the Internet, it appears that most use of Email is made from teachers' home computers. Many teachers choose to carry out administrative tasks at home and it is here that the latest Government initiative of supporting teachers in purchasing their own computers (NGfL, 2000) may reap rewards.

The paper has demonstrated that the structures are in place to support the intended outcomes of training teachers in ICT (TTA, 1998a) and the four benefits detailed in the EDSI report (DfEE, 1997) that relate to administrative uses of ICT. Many more sites could have been mentioned as they do offer support to classroom teachers by way of resources, lesson plans, schemes of work, work sheets, assignments, discussion forums, and on-line activities for pupils. However, reviewing sites is not the purpose of this paper and is an impossible task as there are so many. There has undoubtedly been an explosion of educational sites over the last two years with LEAs, schools and even supermarkets (http://www.tesco.schoolnet2000.com/) providing educational web sites. There are, however, problems that must not be overlooked. Teachers will not use the NGfL or Internet unless they have access to hardware and are confident and competent to do so. The UK Government's schemes for improving the infrastructure and hardware in schools will go some way to meeting their aims. More important is the teacher training aspect and this has been problematic in the past (Selwood, 1999). However, the latest government initiative of supporting teachers in purchasing their own computers (NGfL, 2000), coupled with the current training initiatives (much of which involves the use of the Internet), may resolve the situation. It will have been noted in reading this that all government plans end in 2002 – the date of the next general election. Without continued government funding after the next election those sites, and schools' connections to the Internet, currently supported through public money will not survive, the impetus will be lost and targets not maintained.

REFERENCES

British Educational Communications and Technology Agency. (1998). *Connecting schools – Networking people*. Coventry: Becta.

British Educational Communications and Technology Agency. (1999). *Connecting schools – Networking people 2000*. Coventry: Becta.

British Educational Communications and Technology Agency. (2000). http://www.becta.org.uk/about/whatisbecta.html

Department for Education. (1995). *Superhighways for education*. London: HMSO.

Department for Education and Employment. (1995). *Superhighways for education: The way forward*. London: HMSO.

Department for Education and Employment. (1997a). *Preparing for the information age: A synoptic report for the Education Departments' Superhighways Initiative*. DfEE, London. [http://vtc.ngfl.gov.uk/reference/edsi]

Department for Education and Employment. (1997b). *Connecting the learning society: National Grid for Learning* (Government Consultation Paper). London: DfEE.

Department for Education and Employment. (1998). *Teachers: Meeting the challenge of change*. London: DfEE. [http://www.dfee.gov.uk/teachers/greenpaper/index.htm]

Department for Education and Employment. (1999). *Survey of information and communications technology in schools 1998*. London: DfEE. [http://www.dfee.gov.uk/ict/index.htm]

McKinsey & Company. (1997). *The future of information technology in UK schools*. London: McKinsey and Company. [http://www.rubble.ultralab.anglia.ac.uk/stevenson/McKinsey.html]

National Grid for Learning. (1999). http://www.managedservices.ngfl.gov.uk/communicator.html

National Grid for Learning. (2000). http://cft.ngfl.gov.uk/

Selwood, I. (1999). The development of ICT in secondary education in England and Wales. In A. Jimoyiannis (Ed.), *Panhellenic Conference: Information technology and education.* Ioannina: Association of IT Teachers of Greece.

Selwyn, N. (1999). Successfully establishing a 'National Grid for Learning': Have we been here before? *Computer Education, 93*, 2-8.

Stevenson Committee. (1997). *Information and communications technology in UK schools: An independent enquiry* (The Stevenson Report). London: Pearson. [http://www.rubble.ultralab.anglia.ac.uk/stevenson/ contents.html]

Teacher Training Agency. (1998b). *The National Curriculum for Initial Teacher Training – Annex B (ICT).* London: DfEE. [http://www.teach-tta.gov.uk/ict.thm]

Teacher Training Agency. (1998a). *New Opportunities Fund. The use of ICT in subject teaching lottery-funded training. Expected outcomes.* London: DfEE.

APPENDIX 1 - VIRTUAL TEACHER CENTRES

Table 2. UK virtual teacher centres

Country	
England	http://vtc.ngfl.gov.uk/
Ireland	http://www.nine.org.uk/
Scotland	http://www.svtc.org.uk/
Wales	http://vtccymru.ngfl.wales.gov.uk/